Passive Income:

Start a Digital Business, Make Money Online and Work from Home

Brendan Mace

Table of Contents

Introduction

This book is for people that want to build passive income.

Honestly, that should be just about anyone.

Hate your job?
Hate your boss?
Want freedom?
Want to provide?
Want a vacation?

If you can answer yes to any of those questions, then passive income is something that can transform your life.

Let's put it this way, what would $10,000 per month do to change your living conditions?

I can tell you what it's done for me.

Eight years ago, I stumbled onto one of those bullshit "make money online" advertisements.

Sure, the idea was thrilling, but the information was untrustworthy at best – downright spam at worst.

But it got me thinking, surely someone knows how to make passive income online.

So I searched.

After eight years of scouring every nook and cranny of the internet, I finally have a good idea about what works.

And you know the best part?

I actually make money online. You can look at my income reports at my website: http://www.brendanmace.com

In my recent January income report, I broke $10,000 for that month.

And pretty much every month around that is close to that number. A bad month for me is $7,000 or less. And my numbers continue to grow.

Want to know how I do it?

I figured as much.

Read through this book and you will learn what I do to make over $7,000 every month online.

Whether you want to provide for your family, or you just want a luxurious vacation from the daily grind, I can show you how to change your life.

Enjoy the book!

Regards,

Brendan Mace

Free Bonus

As a small token of thanks for getting this book, I'd like to give you a full course on how to make passive income online.

This training could easily be sold for $100's of dollars.

And in fact, people pay me significant amounts of money to show them how to make money online.

I'm willing to give you a slice of that freedom pie here.

Just visit this page, and learn my powerful Two Step Formula:

http://twostep.brendanmace.com

Part 1:

Part 2:

Part 3:

Find this Bonus Here: http://TwoStep.BrendanMace.com

This bonus is a 3-part video series that shows the process I've used to reach over $8,000/month.

In reality, my income since creating this video series continues to increase. I am happily expecting to make well over "Five Figures Per Month" on a consistent basis.

Whether you like reading or watching a video, I have you covered. My personal preference is to do both, and I recommend you use whatever learning style helps you the most.

I have an entire YouTube channel with 90+ videos on "making money online"

Over 19,000 people are subscribed to my channel, and many have figured this game out.

Join my YouTube tribe here: https://youtube.com/user/macbr9

Chapter 1 – What Are Your Options?

There are many ways to make money online.

This book is going to focus on <u>five of them</u>. Any more than that, and I would worry that your thoughts will be too fragmented. Any less than that, and you may not find a suitable option to get started.

All of these methods can work wonders – as long as you put in the effort on the front end. I have personally used each one, and they all contribute to my $8,000 per month passive income.

What qualifies as passive income?

Don't expect zero work.

You will have to put some effort in at the beginning to build your income stream.

Three of the five options are completely passive after that start up phase.

The last two, however, will need a little attention over time.

You may think, "but Brendan, that's not passive."

I disagree.

A minimal amount of maintenance might not be 'work-free,' but it's still classifiable as passive.

I didn't call this book "Deadbeat Income."

Alas, if you don't want any work involved, you can focus your time on the next three chapters.

Options that are 100% passive

- Niche Websites
- YouTube Publishing
- EBook Publishing

Options that are "mostly" passive

- Blogging
- List Building

The last one is my personal favourite, and makes the most money.

You'll probably heard "the money is in the list"

Well that's true.

There's no way around it. Email marketing can be the most lucrative thing you do online. As far as work goes, it really takes me about ten minutes per day to maintain.

I would call that passive. And since it's my biggest earner, I feel obligated to include it in this fine book.

The one thing you don't hear, but should, is that "the money is all over the place."

You don't need to do list building to make five-figures per month.

You do have options.

Which is the point of this chapter.

Another great one is to become a publisher of some sort.

Sure, there is work involved to publish in the first place. But once your creations are available on each platform, traffic and money can roll in without any additional work involved.

I've done this successfully with niche websites, YouTube and EBook publishing.

When I started eight years ago, my focus was micro niche sites.

I built these up to a very good income stream.

And then one day, Google started releasing updates named after fuzzy little creatures.

You've probably heard of them.

- The Penguin Update

- The Panda Update

- The Ditzy Unicorn Update

Okay, I made that last one up.

But the first two were catastrophic. A lot of people lost their shirt online, and had to start all over again.

Fortunately for me, many of my niche websites are still alive and kicking today. In the next chapter, I will tell you why.

As for YouTube publishing, I now have over 19,000 subscribers.

That means that for every video I release, thousands of people get a notification about it.

This can mean a much better chance of going viral for "Online Marketing" videos.

But you got this book for passive.

Creating new videos is not that.

So instead, let me show you the benefits of having a YouTube channel that could just sit there and roll in more visits than a Super Bowl stadium.

Think about that for a second. My channel has grossed over a million views, and steadily brings in about the same amount of traffic every, single day.

I won't waste your time with more expectation setting.

Let's dive in to your options!

Chapter 2 – Create a Niche Website

In the world of niche sites, there's an annoying little myth that discourages actual progress.

The myth is that the more sites you build, the more you'll make.

In reality, the truth is actually the exact opposite.

Why micro niche sites are a leftover myth from another era?

This chapter is not going to say niche sites are bad.

I've promoted niche sites for years. I even give away EIGHT of my best niche ideas here: http://www.brendanmace.com/8-easy-niches-for-an-amazon-affiliate-your-shortcut/

The PROBLEM is that too many of us are doing it all wrong.

There's this fascinatingly attractive idea to set up a website, throw up some posts, and expect money to pour in like sweat dripping from a sumo wrestler.

That's not the way it works.

And after reading this chapter, you'll understand why.

Who Started the Big Lie?

Actually, no one is to blame for this.

It's just outdated.

When I started with niche sites, about 7 and 1/2 years ago, setting up micro niche sites worked.

It was easy to stumble on the idea.

WarriorForum had famously popular threads on the topic.

Here's one that broke 100K views:

It was a beautiful thing then.

You'd do your good ol' keyword research.

That was key, and continues to be important to this day.

The process was:

- Find a good keyword

- Set up a website

- Write or buy 4-5 posts

- Repeat

Smart marketers repeated this over and over.

And they made money.

So what's the problem?

Those posts that inspired me 7 years ago still exist.

And what's worse: people still read them.

There's a new Joe Blogger every day. Most think a few posts and a good keyword is gonna be life changer.

A follower messaged me last week and said he registered THIRTY domains.

He now plans to create niche sites on all of them.

Hate to cut the sails down before the shipwreck, but that's just emotional suicide.

None of those thirty sites will make more than $10/month.

That's the truth.

So what's the real way to build a niche site?

This may seem rather obvious.

If puny niche sites are swallowed up by the vast Google wastelands, then clearly you should create a non-puny niche site.

BINGO...

It actually doesn't really even need to be a "niche" site per se. As long as your site features lots of juicy quality stuff, it will fare much better with the G-bot.

Follow these simple steps, and you will create a site that withstands all future updates.

Step #1 — More than Four Pages

What quality site has less than 20 pages?

Can you think of one?

Not possible, right?

Sites like Amazon, Ebay, NyTimes, etc all have thousands of pages.

Google is not stupid.

A site with less than a couple dozen pages will not be an authority — Nor should it be.

Lots of pages is crucial.

Step #2 — Visitors Enjoy the Site

It would be easy to publish garbage.

You could buy it for $5 a pop on Fiverr. Or you could use some crappy Auto Post 3000 software to make some steamy content goop.

That's not gonna work.

But Brendan, Google is not a human. It can't read webpages and test for quality.

AHHHH… But that's where you're wrong, laddy.

Google can't read the pages, but it can see how fellow humans are digesting it.

This is also known as "user metrics"

There's three crucial "how's"

- How long does a visitor stay

- How many pages does a visitor see

- How often does a visitor 'bounce'

The first two are obvious.

If you're curious about "bounce rate," it means does the visitor immediately leaves after seeing your site.

A crappy website will lose visitors faster than a smelly fart.

So yes, Google will know if your site sucks.

Step #3 — Updates on a Reasonable Basis

This is a bit of a changer.

While you could leave a site without updates for years, it's now more important to keep adding more.

And it makes sense.

Let's think again, what quality site would _____?

In this case we're asking "what site would stop updating?"

Not always the case, but usually this indicates a lack of authority.

Good sites are maintained.

Skipping this step is a big red flag to Google.

Step #4 — Real Social Love

Without question, you could fake this one.

The idea is that if a site is good, people will share it with their friends.

There are ways to get social shares that are self-contrived.

The only problem I have with getting fake social signals is that it's unsustainable.

Sure, you may have the time and energy to fake it for awhile, but do you really want to regularly fake shares?

On top of that, do you want to balance out the shares, so that they appear real?

…Of course not.

That would be a HUGE dump of your time.

The whole goal of a niche site is that it's passive or mostly passive.

That means any social signals need to be sustainable.

There's one real easy way to get more shares…

… ASK FOR THEM.

A quality site could double its social signals, simply by ending pages with a genuine plead for likes

Something simple, like "If you enjoyed my review of ____, please share it with your friends."

A whole three second task, and it would immensely improve your sharing.

Another great way is to start a social following on the big networks.

I've shown how to do that on:

- Pinterest
- Twitter
- Tumblr
- FaceBook

It's easier than you think.

An Action Plan — For Do'ers

Nothing equals nothing.

Take no action and you will get nowhere.

So let's set the right plan of attack.

1. Pick something you're passionate about

2. Research keyword possibilities — Go or No?

3. Can you turn this into an authority site — Go or No?

4. Write or Outsource quality pages. Personality helps.

5. Build it out over time.

6. Grow a following via social networks, email list, etc.

Sound easy enough?

Now go do it!

Chapter 3 – YouTube Publishing

In 2017, Cisco estimates that 67% of web traffic will be <u>video content.</u> Not only are videos much easier to create than long-winded articles, they're also consumed with a higher retention rate.

Most people don't read…

Other than Facebook, Twitter, Tumblr, etc., most visitors will spend only a few seconds on text-based content before clicking the "back" button, or moving on to something else (likely a video).

Video, on the other hand, retains visitors for longer. And in general, is much easier at getting traffic in the first place. Even though articles are quickly losing their grasp on visitor attention, there are also many more articles on the inter-webs than videos.

In other words, <u>less videos</u> are getting <u>a LOT</u> more traffic.

Convinced yet?

What do I know about making videos?

In the <u>last 30 days,</u> my <u>YouTube videos</u> have been seen over 72,000 times.

This is not to brag. But creating only 80 videos, and receiving that kind of traffic, would be unheard of with a comparable amount of articles. That's almost a thousand sets of eyeballs per video (on average).

Not to mention, these views are all in the highly competitive "make money online" space.

Even better results (numbers-wise) could be had in LOADS of other niches.

What can you do with video traffic?

You have lots of options with video.

You can:

- Collect leads

- Make affiliate sales

- AdSense revenue

- Branding

- Website promotion

Pretty much anything you can do with a blog, you can do with a video.

How to Create your Videos

Making videos is easy. To start, you have a few options.

- Talking head
- Slideshow
- Screen Capture

A brief explanation of each:

1) Talking Head- Person(s) in front of a camera. Discussing a niche-related topic.

2) Slideshow- A series of slides or animations with a voice over.

3) Screen Capture- the speaker records screen while giving instructions.

In my opinion, the video style you choose should depend on your niche.

My favourite, and the style I use the most, is Slideshow or Screen Capture

A screen recording with voiceover sounds as boring as cats, but with the tools on the market today, you can easily make a *snazzy* looking video that both impresses and earns sales.

People eat these vids up... And with a *step-by-step* format, it's very realistic to get eyeballs to engage and take action on your videos. This is CRUCIAL in making sales.

You can see the screen capture videos I create, right here.

How to create these videos?

You can do this entire stuff 100% for free, and in the next few minutes with a tool called Microsoft Expression Encoder.

You will have some limitations with this tool, though.

First off, you're only able to record 10 minutes max. For many of us – that's a problem.

And it lacks *features* you'll get with a premium tool.

Always got to give a shout out to Microsoft for making Expression Encoder free. Not all of us have a budget to use on a video-editing tool.

If you do have even a tiny amount of cash to invest, then you absolutely should get a premium tool.

What you should buy!

There are dozens of video creation tools on the market. All of them feature their own perks and have their own drawbacks.

The learning curve is very high for most of them.

VideoMakerFX is the video creator that I recommend the most to newbies – because it's easy to use, and creates some *really badass* videos.

Its focus is slideshow vids with cool animations. Take a look here!

This is an especially good option for people that prefer not to show their face on camera. I remember starting my own video creation in the beginning. I refused to show my face – I was too damn shy. This tool would have been a godsend back then.

VideoMakerFX has everything you need, for less than $97…

Here's what you get…

Most other video creators either cost WAYYY Too much money, or offer no online support for their products.

VideoMakerFX offers top-notch online support, and is priced very reasonably.

How many people are using VideoMakerFX?

One concern about software tools (in general) is future updates. The problem with many of these software programs is that once the product creator's made the moola, they have no incentive to keep their customers happy – they move on to the next shiny object.

VideoMakerFX has sold over 29,500 copies… It's not going away. You can confidently expect future updates for many years. You may not realize how important that is… Lots of these video tools come and go… You can have full confidence that this will be here for good.

It's actually the #1 selling product of all-time on JvZoo. Forget the "product of the day" awards. This one's the best seller… Ever!

Okay, okay Brendan…

It's the best seller of all time on JvZoo. Beating out all the other alternatives. That's pretty impressive.

So far, I know that:

- It's easy to use (unlike most alternatives)

- It creates high quality slideshow videos

- It includes background music

- It includes tons of background images

- Also comes with 140+ animation slides

I also know that video is literally the way of the future.

In less than a decade, over 60% of web traffic will be to videos.

So I should create videos, if I want to be successful from here on out.

This is the easiest, and most impressive video tool under $200.

…

==> Grab Your Copy While it's Still on Special <==

You'll be able to throw together simple YouTube vids in the next few minutes.

Making the Most from YouTube

The traffic numbers you can get from YouTube is absolutely outrageous!

Right now, I'm getting about 3,100 visitors per day, and it continues to climb every week.

What would you do with that much traffic?

- Redirect them to your blog

- Get email subscribers

- Make affiliate commissions

- Quit your job

With the traffic you can get from YouTube, you could easily make a comfortable living in no time.

HOWEVER

There are a couple things you have to know.

1. Your videos can't be pointless

2. You need to promote them

Your videos are POINTLESS if they do not get more fans to your channel or make you affiliate commissions with product placement.

At the beginning, your priority should be about growing your fan base and getting more views on your videos.

There are TWO main ways to grow your channel

- Email List

- YouTube Organic

Growing an email list (highly recommended) is like having traffic on tap. At any time – send visitors to whatever you want. In other words… having a list could be more like having money on tap.

Of course, you'll send a lot of your email traffic to affiliate promotions, or traffic exchanges. That's where you can make some REAL BIG MOOLA.

Still, sending visitors to video is an excellent opportunity to build trust with your subscribers, while growing your YouTube channel at the same time.

I like to mix in a few video promotions per week to my mailing list. I send emails daily. To get on my list, go here.

I have no real hard data that proves my email-to-video promotions are impactful. These have helped me grow my channel a lot, though. Your email subs are some of your biggest fans. Showing them what you're doing on YouTube is going to be well received by them.

To learn how to grow an email list fast. I have a full step-by-step guide here: How to Build a List Fast

With your email list — you'll have traffic forever!

Growing the Organic Way

YouTube is a search engine, just like Google.com

Getting organic traffic from YouTube is as simple as ranking in their search listings.

OR… an easier way, is to be listed in their related vids sidebar -- more on that later. It's UBER powerful, and is used by the better YouTube marketers.

Let's get back…

Cracking the YouTube Algorithm

In order to reach the top spots of YouTube search, you need to impress the YouTube algorithm.

Let's be clear… Google owns YouTube.

That means that the algorithm for YouTube operates the SAME way.

YouTube's algorithm has metrics (things it pays attention to). Get the best #'s on YouTube's metrics, and the top spot is yours. It's that simple.

Let's talk about the metrics!

How YouTube Ranks Videos?

There are 5 main factors for YouTube ranking.

- • Optimization – Video title, description, tags, etc.

- • Engagement – Likes, shares, comments, embeds, etc.

- • Retention – How long viewers are watching…

- • Authority – Channel views, subscribers, etc.

- • # of Views – Self-explanatory. # of views on the video.

Video optimization is *easy* to master. It's a simple science of picking the search term(s) you want ranked, and then selecting a title and description that focus on that term(s).

Engagement on your vids is important. A simple way to increase your likes, shares and comments is to ask (in-video) for them. Sounds stupidly simple – but it works!

Retention rate is a crucial metric. In short, it's how long your visitors watch your video. Full watch-throughs will improve this metric. Cutting out before midway will seriously impede your video's rank. Retention is life or death. You WILL NOT rank without a good score.

There are a few tricks to improve retention. In general, though, the quality of your video matters most. Videos that use humor, curiosity, or legitimately stimulate viewers will usually have higher retention rates.

Authority is a reward to channel owners that consistently create high retention videos. This will not be granted overnight – it's a growing gift that increases as you publish more quality videos. My channel started with zero authority – now my videos get ranked much more easily than before.

# of views is much easier when you already have ranked videos or channel authority. Without the luxury of having an established channel, you'll have to work a bit harder to get this one improved. Sharing videos on social networks or mailing to your list are two great ways to get more views. Something to think about…

Those are the 5 main factors in YouTube's algorithm. The last two are usually going to take some time for new YouTubers — the first three are what you should focus on.

Getting your videos ranked organically is a lot of free traffic.

Once you have an established YouTube channel (like mine), organic rankings will come a lot easier.

Keyword Research

This is the same as finding keywords for a blog post. Your best bet is to use Google Keyword Planner, or if you have some spare change, invest in LongTailPro.

I created keyword research tutorials here, here and here.

… Let's start from scratch, though. This'll be quick.

Go to Google Keyword Planner.

Click on the button shown in the image below.

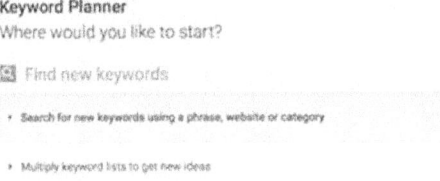

Once you click on "Search for new keywords…"

You'll get this drop down

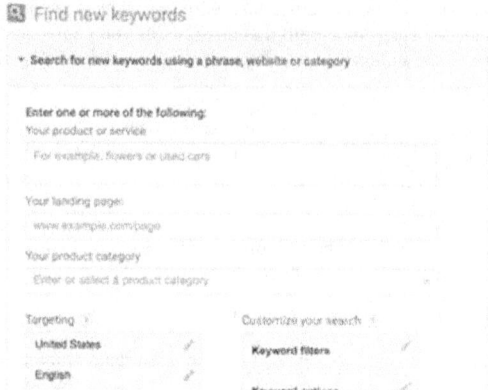

Now you just need to fiddle around for a few minutes and find some seed keyword ideas.

Examples of seed keywords:

- Affiliate marketing

- Link building

- Get traffic

- Create a blog

- Keyword research

Once you get your seed keywords, now plug them into YouTube search and see what results pop up.

For example…

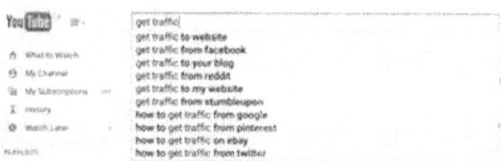

From this quick method – I can see a few GREAT keyword opportunities.

- Get Traffic to Your Blog

- Get Traffic from Reddit

- Get Traffic to My Website

• How to Get Traffic from Google

There is a SIMPLE method to getting more views. Even for high authority channels I'm about to share the #1 best way to get video views — it's not organic search.

YouTube Siphon Hack

There is a traffic source that trumps organic search. It's called "<u>suggested videos</u>," and it can be massive.

Here's a look at my YouTube traffic sources.

Traffic source ⓘ	Views ⓘ ▾	Estimated minutes watched ⓘ	Average views ⓘ duration
Suggested videos ⓘ	28,550 (49%)	752,129 (30%)	2.56
YouTube search	21,263 (37%)	74,749 (24%)	3.90
Browse on playlistpage ⓘ	5,546 (7%)	19,805 (4.5%)	3.34
External ⓘ	5,306 (6.4%)	19,593 (5%)	3.99
YouTube channel page	4,239 (1.4%)	20,606 (4.9%)	4.55
Browse features ⓘ	1,997 (2.3%)	9,078 (2.5%)	4.32
Playlists	932 (1.2%)	4,354 (1.4%)	4.32
Video cards and annotations	747 (0.9%)	4,166 (1.4%)	5.34
Other YouTube features	424 (0.5%)	1,918 (0.6%)	4.30
Notifications	18 (0.0%)	118 (0.0%)	6.37
YouTube advertising ⓘ	4 (0.0%)	11 (0.0%)	10.34

My traffic from suggested videos almost DOUBLES YouTube search. And that's analytics from a channel with a dozen or so <u>ranked videos</u>. As a newbie, suggested videos are even MORE important. This is your video goldmine.

What can you do to get more Suggested Views?

Do a quick <u>YouTube search</u> for relevant keywords. ← Do not worry about organic search competition. With this method, we are not trying to rank our video. We are getting our video to show up on the right sidebar for videos that are already ranking.

For example…

Let's say we decided on the keyword "how to make money with YouTube"

Here are the videos that are currently ranking:

You'll notice:

• The #1 ranked video has over 800,000 views.

• The #2 ranked video has over 350,000 views.

We're not going to try and outrank these videos. Maybe one day… But right now, these are exceptionally high quality videos created by channels that have WAYY more authority than ours!

Instead, we want to be the video that shows up on the sidebar for one of these videos.

Like this:

How To Make Money On YouTube (4 Simple Strategies)

I put a red circle around one of the suggested vids.

Notice how most of these sidebar videos have 700,000+ views...

That's almost (and in some cases, more) views than the top ranked video.

Clearly, getting to the top spots of these suggested videos is very valuable.

How to do it!

The algorithm for suggested videos is very simple.

- Video Similarity

- Video Quality

There are a few other factors – but these are the main two.

Video Similarity is the <u>MOST</u> important factor. We're going to maximize our chance of getting suggested traffic by making our video as similar as possible to already ranking videos.

In other words...

We're going to find out:

- The title of ranking videos

- The description

- A brief look at the video content

- Lastly, the tags of the video

Then, we're going to optimize our video's title, description, content and tags. So that it's very close – but different – to the ranking video.

Let's look at the top ranking video again...

The first three factors are easy to find and emulate. <u>Video Tags</u> are a little harder to uncover – they're the secret sauce to claiming your spot, though. So pay attention!

Title = How to Make Money on YouTube (4 Simple Strategies)

Description = In this video, James Wedmore discusses the FOUR simple strategies for actually monetizing your efforts on YouTube.com. However, even though James mentions FOUR strategies, he only recommends one… the last one… (Continued…)

Content = James is talking about 4 strategies that you can use to make money from YouTube.

Video Tags = I bolded the title of "video tags" cause this is easily the most important of the bunch. You've probably heard at one point or another that tags are insignificant. That may be true when it comes to Google Search – YouTube's algorithm is different. It relies on <u>video tags</u> to understand what the video is about…

Why is this the case?

Google spiders cannot enter videos. It's a geeky story – just trust me, though. Google spiders can easily whip through text-based content in no time. When a G-bot runs into a video, it skips over it, and looks at any other indicators to decide the content.

So video tags are literally a conversation piece to the YouTube algorithm. You're telling it exactly what your video is all about. This is where you want to have to tags similar to our target video.

How to Find Video Tags

The easiest way to find YouTube tags is to use <u>this chrome extension.</u>

Here's the step-by-step:

- Open up Google Chrome (or download it)

- Go to <u>http://vidiq.com/apps/vision/</u>

- Go to YouTube and pick video to uncover tags

- Make sure you're logged into Vision

- Video Tags on right sidebar

If you completed this process, you should see a box that looks like this…

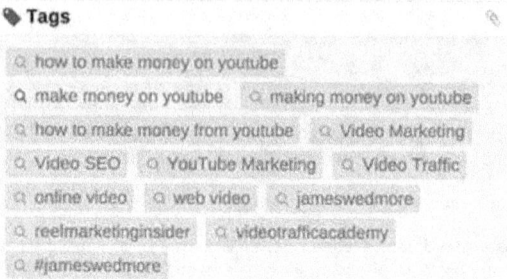

Tags

- how to make money on youtube
- make money on youtube
- making money on youtube
- how to make money from youtube
- Video Marketing
- Video SEO
- YouTube Marketing
- Video Traffic
- online video
- web video
- jameswedmore
- reelmarketinginsider
- videotrafficacademy
- #jameswedmore

Pretty cool, huh?

These are the video tags for the #1 ranking video on "How to Make Money on YouTube"

My advice is to copy 60% of these tags and paste them unchanged into your video.

Then find another similar video with a good amount of views, and copy 20%-50% of its tags.

Finally, create 5-10 original tags, one of which is your channel name (more on this later...)

By simply focusing on:

- Similar tags
- Descriptions
- Title
- Content

You are increasing your chance of being the #1 suggested vid

When you go to YouTube, how many videos do you watch?

Chances are, you watch more than one video. The suggested video sidebar gets used ALL THE TIME.

The slogan for YouTube, could easily be "bet ya can't watch just one"

The average user watches 3+ videos on EACH session.

That's why it's so powerful to have your video in the sidebar.

One More Advanced U-Tube Trick for even MORE Traffic

There's one more way to use video tags to get more traffic.

Take a look here:

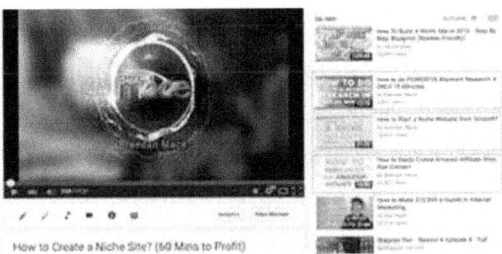

How to Create a Niche Site? (60 Mins to Profit)

This is one of my videos on How to Create a Video Niche Site

For what I'm about to show you – I could have chosen ANY of my videos.

Basically, you want to create a tag for ALL of your videos that is UNIQUE to YOU.

The tag I use is "Brendan Mace"

You'll notice that I have THREE suggested videos above the fold. That's more than half of all videos showing in the sidebar.

Really simple:

- • My video showing includes my unique tag: "Brendan Mace"
- • My suggested videos also include tag: "Brendan Mace"

For every video I create, I include this tag. This increases the odds of YouTube including MY VIDEOS in the suggested sidebar.

So if the average user watches 3+ videos in a single session. There is a damn good chance they'll watch 2+ of my videos, if they view a vid on my channel.

Pretty cool, huh?

Those two advanced YouTube marketing secrets alone have OUTRAGEOUSLY increased my popularity.

If I can do it – so can you!

Making Cash

You can get all the traffic in the world, but you won't make a penny without monetizing it.

The easiest form of monetization also happens to be the least lucrative.

Monetizing with AdSense – Should you do it?

To make money with AdSense on YouTube – All you have to do is become a YouTube Partner and activate ads on all your videos.

This one's tough... Most marketers are on one side of the fence, or the other.

James Wetmore claims that AdSense monetization is a waste, and there are more lucrative ways to make money from YouTube videos.

That's 100% true. There are better ways to make FAT STACKS from YouTube.

The question is... Should you do both?

I use YouTube AdSense for a several hundred-dollar income stream (not allowed to reveal any exact figures).

I make WAYY more with product placement links. I'm happy with some extra hundreds every month, though. In the end, it's all up to you!

Making the Real FAT STACKS on YouTube – What Most are Missing!

The best way to make money with YouTube is actually a fairly untapped strategy. It's using in-video annotations to direct traffic to affiliate products.

Be CAREFUL!

There's a good way to do this...

Take a look at this video.

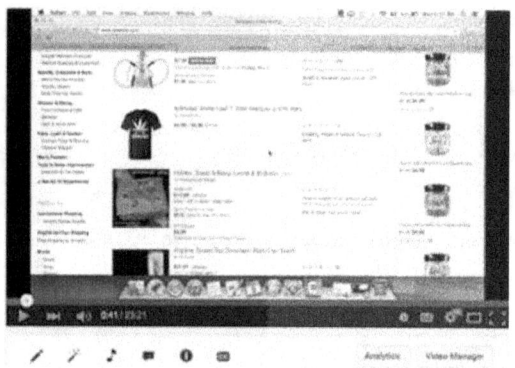

Create a Profitable Niche Site In 20 Mins (Covert Theme)

In this video, I shared a full 23-minute tutorial on how to create a niche site

Watch the video – you'll notice the promotion complements the tutorial.

You want to give away LOADS of value for two reasons.

   1 Your vids will not be considered spammy

   2 Your vids will get WAYY more exposure (people will actually share them)

Most marketers get a little lazy here, and tell viewers to click a link in the description.

That's an all right strategy – you will make some sales.

The BETTER option is to have video annotations.

Your CTR is WAYY higher with in-video annotation. Lemme show ya how to do that.

How to Create In-Video Annotations – For MAX CTR

First off – you need to actually be a YouTube partner to use annotations. Which is valuable for many reasons. Become one ASAP!

— I created a video on how to do this —=" blank">Try watching this video on www.youtube.com</a>, or enable JavaScript if it is disabled in your browser.</div></div>

Getting annotations for your videos is UBER important. Be sure to do this – your results will be much better.

The one question you likely have at this point… is so what, annotations can only be sent to associated website links.

Ahhhhhhh…

Good question – you're 100% right.

Annotations can only link to your site – we have a nice little workaround, though…

To direct traffic to affiliate products, or anything for that matter – you just need to create redirect links on your website.

A good tool for this is called PrettyLink

The Lite Version (which is all you need) can host links on your site that direct to ANY address you want.

Cool eh?

So for example…

You could have a link on your site that's www.yoursite.com/anything

That link could *technically* be hosted by your site – but will redirect anywhere you want.

And that's EXACTLY how you get away with sending traffic from annotations to anywhere you want.

What Does YouTube Think About This?

They're fine with it. There are many YouTube publishers that use this exact strategy to get traffic to where they want. It's 100% TOS compliant.

However!

YouTube does care about "low quality content" that's SOLELY created to get visitors to affiliate links.

This is, again, where my insistence on quality videos is important.

With high quality videos, YouTube is happy to help you be successful.

You want to work with YouTube – not against them.

Nuggets of Wisdom

Remember earlier we discussed the importance of video engagement and views.

How many times your video is embedded and/or shared on FB and Twitter has an impact on your video rankings.

Here's a list of what YouTube looks for....

77.9 Views Per Hour	**3.2M** Minutes Watched	**826.2K** Views
38 Embedded Sources	**80.8K** Channel Subscribers	**434** Youtube Shares 0.1% of views
5,872 Subscribers Driven 0.7% of views	**106** FB Likes 0.0% of views	**242** FB Shares 0.0% of views
45 FB Comments 0.0% of views	**11K** YouTube Likes	**1,388** YouTube Dislikes
300 Tweets 0.0% of views	**3,673** Google +1's	**1** StumbleUpon Views 0.0% of views
3 LinkedIn Count	**10** Desc Link Count	**235** Desc Word Count
156.5 Words Per Minute	**1/19** Creator Suggested	**2.0%** True Engagement Rate

Includes lots of social behavior:

FB likes/comments, Tweets, Google +1's, YouTube shares/likes.

… And Embeds.

Hmmmmmm…

How can we get this ball rolling?

Embeds are where you share the video on another website.

It's easy – Copy the embed code and enter the code into another site.

It looks like this:

When you embed the video on your site, it'll show up as a full YouTube video, hosted on your website.

Not only will you get extra video views (a ranking factor), it'll also count as an embed source (also a ranking factor).

So TWO ranking boosts, all in one go…

Pretty damn cool.

Where else can we embed our vids?

I like to create video niche sites where I publish ALL my YouTube videos.

They look like this one here: http://macevidz.com

Every single one of my videos gets an additional embed – as well as shares, views, etc.

The theme I use for this is called CovertVideoPress

I love this theme for the embeds – but it's also exceptional at getting FB likes and social shares.

Here's a quick look:

Take a look at the bottom left…

There's a "like" and "share" button.

These work because they're located right where YouTube's like and share buttons would be…

Except in this case, visitors like the video on FACEBOOK instead of YouTube.

Which will also work to distribute the video to all their friends.

And get even more exposure to your video(s).

Where else can we share?

Another great option is on all your social networks.

Facebook, Pinterest, Twitter, Tumblr, Social Blogs, Etc.

With most of these networks, you just need to post the URL of the video, and they'll take care of the code for you.

This will get ya an extra embed – and with some FB friends, you could even get a few Facebook likes and views.

Here's an example:

Easy, right?

That's a simple way to boost your traffic and shares.

Cheap Outsourcing for Quicker Results – Fiverr is Your Friend

Fiverr is a site that sells things for $5.

There are a few things you should buy that will REALLY ramp things up.

- Video intro
- Video outro
- Channel art
- Video thumbnails
- Social bookmarks

A video intro and channel art is an important professional touch.

When viewers check out your channel – they are way more likely to subscribe if you're channel looks like a million bucks.

All in – channel art and a video intro will cost ya 10 bucks.

There's NO REASON to skip this step. It's the cheapest way to add a TON of subscribers and views to your bottom line.

Go to Fiverr and search for "video intro" and "YouTube header"

A video outro is important for three reasons:

1 Looks professional

2 Subscriber collector

3 Related views

Similar to the intro, it's a nice touch to your videos.

It ALSO has the function of getting more subscribers and related views.

Here's a look at my outro:

It includes links to other videos on my channel.

Most importantly – it has the "Subscribe" button.

These are all connected to video annotations. So when visitors click on the buttons, they actually perform the appropriate tasks.

This is an awesome way to collect a bunch of extra leads and views.

You should do this!

Video thumbnails are crucial for more views

Part of the YouTube algorithm (not yet discussed) is CTR.

When your video shows up in search or in the suggested videos, you need people to actually CLICK on the thumbnail of your video.

By default, YouTube will take a snapshot of the middle of your video, and use it as the thumbnail.

The better option is to submit a custom thumbnail.

You could make this yourself.

Cause I'm lazy – and want it done professionally. I spend… you guessed it… $5 to get all my thumbnails done on Fiverr.

Check them out here: Brendan Mace's YouTube Channel

All those thumbnails cost me $5 a piece.

That's a steal – in my opinion.

Social bookmarks will boost your YouTube and Google rankings.

You could do social bookmarking all manually.

OR, you could get hundreds of bookmarks for $5.

For example:

A few hundred social bookmarks will improve your video seo.

Social bookmarks are optional – these can all be earned manually.

Adding some additional one's through Fiverr is not a bad idea, though.

And cheap!

The Results

Here's a quick look at my YouTube stats (last 30 days)

In the last month – 336,626 minutes = 234 days worth of viewing time.

Imagine how many sales you could make with that viewing time.

It's easy:

- Get VideoMakerFX to create videos
- Optimize your videos for engagement
- Pick the right keywords
- Use video tags to steal competitors traffic
- Video annotations for maximum sales
- Embed videos on other sites/networks
- Use Fiverr for cheap, professional designs

That's everything I know about video marketing. My YouTube channel makes me about $2k/month on complete autopilot.

Once you have this stuff up and running – you can relax.

Travel the world. Live your life!

Chapter 4 – EBook Publishing

You can create and publish a book in the next 24 hours that will pay you out for years to come.

There are two ways to make money from EBooks

1. Direct sales

2. Links within the book

The convenient thing about EBooks is that people are usually connected to the Internet while reading them.

This gives you a huge opportunity to cash in on affiliate sales and email subscribers, but more on that later.

What topic should you pick?

I'll spare you the ramble about why it needs to be a passion.

You get it.

In order to write a full book, you need to know what you're talking about and it's also best if you actually give a damn. You'll go insane if you try and write a book on a topic that disinterests you. Don't do it!

Getting that passion part out of the way, you'll want to select something that will actually draw an audience.

There are two main websites to look at

1. Smashwords

2. Amazon

What you're looking for is a topic that gets lots of traffic and sales, but isn't oversaturated with books.

I've got one: Organic Lip Balms

That's a topic that people are searching for but isn't overloaded with a ton of competition. As of right now, anyways, maybe after the publication of this book, someone will seize the opportunity.

What if small niches don't interest me?

No problem.

Later I'm going to show you how to get traffic on virtually any topic.

It's exactly why you're reading this book right now in one of the most competitive and saturated topics on the planet.

How many words per book?

Any quality book you publish on Smashwords and Amazon should be at least 6,000 words. It's okay to write a book that length, but any smaller than that and you're likely under-delivering value on your topic.

The book you're reading right now is actually over 20,000 words; to give you some perspective.

What about outsourcing?

Absolutely! You can outsource anything in the book creation process. Go to http://UpWork.com and you'll be able to hire dozens of writers looking for a job.

The rate I look for is around $1 per 100 words.

That may sound cheap, but you can find a quality writer willing to write books at that price point.

What else is involved?

You need a book cover.

And I don't say that lightly. Your book cover and title are the main two things a visitor will see before buying your book.

How it appears visually is super important.

Lucky for you, http://fiver.com has a whole whack of designers creating covers for just five bucks.

If you're determined to do the work yourself, you can use a free service like http://pixlar.com to create a quality cover. Just make sure you use the right dimensions of your cover to add to Smashwords and Amazon.

Why is Smashwords important?

You've almost certainly heard of Amazon. You'd have to be living under a rock to not have heard of them.

You may not have heard about Smashwords, but they're very important.

Smashwords.com will distribute your book to other important online retailers. Sites like Barnes and Noble use Smashwords to fill their book catalogues.

Not to mention Smashwords allows you to publish free books; Amazon only allows free for a limited time (with one exception mentioned later).

It's important to publish your book at both Amazon and Smashwords.

How much do you make from direct sales?

If your book ranks for a mid-to-high traffic topic, you can make lots of sales per month.

I've seen EBook publishers make over $1,000/month from just a handful of books.

But then, it's really a small percentage of books that make most of your money. So it's all about testing and getting stuff out there.

What about high competition topics?

This is something I promised to talk about.

It's an advanced strategy that takes advantage of consumer's desire for free.

When a book is free, it gets lots of "purchases" and a lot of attention.

Sure, you don't make any money directly from book sales, however, if thousands of people are downloading your book, it's easy to make the money back in the links within the book itself.

For example, if I have a book on "list building," I could offer readers a free bonus on that exact topic; maybe a video series on email marketing or some sort of relevant resource guide. The catch is that in order to get that free bonus, readers need to subscribe to my email list.

I can actually give you an example directly in this book. Right now, go to http://twostep.brendanmace.com and you'll get a free internet marketing video series.

See how easy that is?

I'm leveraging the traffic I get from free books to make money within the book itself. It really is a brilliant way to get exposure and sales in the toughest of book topics.

In the last chapter of this book, I'll be sharing list-building secrets in depth. You could easily combine EBook publishing with email marketing to ramp up results into overdrive.

How to make a book free everywhere?

This is a little tricky.

Not all distributers allow you to publish a book for free. Amazon, as an example, only allows you to publish a book for free temporarily: three days max.

There is a workaround, though.

Smashwords allows you to publish your book for free, which gets it sent out to other major retailers like Barnes and Noble.

Once your book is listed for free at a bunch of reputable sources, you can contact the rest and request a price match.

Most retailers will allow your book to be permanently free, in order to price match it with the other guys.

Your Action Plan

1. Write or outsource a book.

2. Create or outsource a cover.

Getting the book created is the first priority. Then it's time to get it out there.

Before you do anything else, you should publish your EBook on Smashwords.com. They'll distribute it to other big retailers.

Then Amazon is a no brainer.

If you already have your book published on other major retailers, Amazon will allow you to price match your book at permanently free.

You have to make your money in one of two ways.

1. Direct sales

2. Links within the book

If it's a niche topic, you can focus on sales directly.

If it's a competitive marketplace with loads of other options, make your book free and bank off the insides of the book.

EBook publishing is a huge opportunity.

Make it happen!

Chapter 5 – Make Money Blogging

The first step to **making money blogging** is to stop searching for "how to make money with blogging." Not because blogging for a living is impossible -- it is a reality for many.

The problem is the stuff you find will mostly 'lose' you money; kind of like asking a casino owner how to make money in Vegas.

Blogging for money is not a hobby. Every guy and his grandma have created a casual blog. The audience for most of these sites extends to family and friend. If they're unlucky, maybe a handful of straggling strangers, stumbling from an obscure Google search, too.

This illusion of making easy money blogging is emboldened by the relatively few examples of bloggers that make six-figures and beyond.

... Or is it an illusion?

Most realists will tell you that blogging cannot make you money. These same people are aware that blogging can make *someone* very wealthy. After all, they have probably read a six-figure blog or two in the past twelve months. They just don't think <u>you</u> can do it.

They want you to be realistic like them.

My goal with this guide is to convince a realist to see the sheer potential of blogging for a living. Not only is it possible, but also if you take the right action as outlined here, making money from blogging is inevitable.

Don't let small minds convince you that your dreams are too big.

Grow your mind, instead.

Getting Started with Blogging

Before cashing any checks, you need a virtual stomping ground.

A website you can call your own.

One of the biggest mistakes newbies make is they choose a free platform.

That's okay if you want a hobby blog.

And I actually show you how to do the hobby blog set up, right here.

If you're serious about blogging, though, you need a self-hosted solution.

How to Set Up Your Website

You'll WASTE years of passive income, if you don't create a website today.

Dead serious.

The #1 mistake in this industry is putting off building your own site.

Hate to be the bringer of bad news. That's the reality.

... Please don't shoot the messenger!

The **GOOD NEWS** is that creating a website is easy.

There are loads of options. Lots of freebie tools. And editors so easy, your grandma could use them.

Where Should You Start?

The first step is to register a domain name.

My personal favourite website for domains is **NameSilo.com (no affiliation)**

Another alternative is **www.namecheap.com**

For this tutorial, we're going to be working with NameSilo.

Go to **this website,** and set up an account. (2 mins approx)

Step #2 is finding a domain name.

If you're struggling with this take **a look at LongTailPro.**

It's a keyword tool that makes it easy to find keywords that get lots of searches.

However, I do not recommend picking a domain name based on the keyword. The idea here is to find a site topic that will have lots of search potential.

Nobody wants to create an entire site, and then find out that nobody cares.

Which is the reality that many of us run into with niche sites.

It may even be worth your while to dive in to an industry.

A site based on:

- Make Money Online

- Health

- Fitness

Is never going to struggle for potential viewers or customers.

The challenge is to get these eyeballs to YOUR site.

We'll cover this later...

For now, head to NameSilo.com and use the Domain finder tool and pick something.

Here's what it'll look like:

You can find this tool right at the homepage.

Very easy to use.

Once you search for a domain name, it'll take you to the next page.

Here's what you'll see:

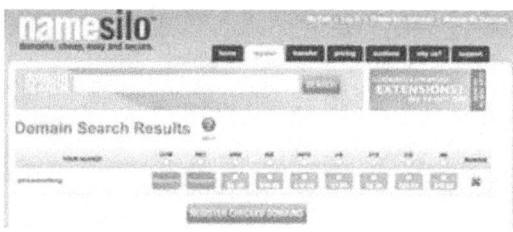

In this case, I chose to search for "picksomething"

The tool is now telling me that:

- picksomething.com

• picksomething.net

But... **PickSomething.org** is still available.

This is where you should make a judgment call.

There is no SEO benefit for having a ".com" website.

There might be branding benefits, though, to having a ".com" domain extension. So I completely understand when people **NEED TO HAVE** a site with a com ending.

In my case, I like having a ".com" or a ".net"

So I'm going to pick something else.

Instead, I've decided on SimpleToBuild.net

That's the domain we'll be working with for the remainder of this action guide.

Step #3 is Getting Hosting for your Domain

Trust me - there's no way around this one.

Yes, you can get a free site set up with Blogger, Wix, Weebly, etc.

But let me ask you this...

Have you seen **anyone** make good money from a free website?

I've been online since 2005, and I've yet to see anybody do it.

Hosting your site is going to cost you about five bucks per month. If you can't do that, I question your dedication or any intention to actually make this work.

You need hosting - get it!

But where?

My favourite place to get hosting is from HostGator

Don't buy it yet!!

Seriously.

First you want an explanation for why to pick them as a host. And then I have a nice HostGator **coupon code** that'll save you a good slice off the final bill.

When I started online in 2005, I tried many different hosting services.

From everything I tried, HostGator was the best:

1. For site speed

2. Up time (almost never down)

3. Overall reliability

Another really good touch is that HostGator support is world class.

They respond nearly instantly, and really help solve any issues.

Having that support could be CRUCIAL if something happens to one of your sites.

And you have to imagine, an issue will probably come up at some point.

HostGator will deal with it for you.

What's the coupon code?

The coupon: **get25offyourbill**

Copy that code, and get ready to use it pretty quick.

First, sign up to a hosting plan on the homepage:

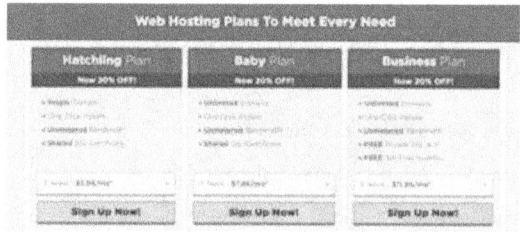

I usually recommend the "Baby Plan"

The Hatchling Plan is too limited. And the Business Plan is unnecessary.

You'll just need to fill out some basic information, and then check off some boxes.

In the next section, they'll ask you about "additional services"

It looks like this:

Never fear - you don't need any of these add-ons.

Uncheck all the boxes and move to the coupon section.

Now you can throw in your **coupon code** and save 25%

Looks like this:

And boom.

That's it.

You now have website hosting.

You're only a couple minutes away from having your own site up and running online.

The LAUNCH - Connecting Your Domain to Hosting

At this point, we have purchased two separate services.

We bought a Domain Name + Web Hosting

Our next step is to connect these two services together.

Log in to NameSilo

Then click on the "Domain Manager" button.

You can find that on the right sidebar.

That will take you to a page with a list of your domains.

My looks like this:

Notice that most of these domains are **hosted with HostGator.**

If you pick the Baby Plan, you are allowed to have unlimited sites. So go crazy.

I recommend focusing on one site at a time. But it's really easy to add more sites to your hosting. And it won't cost you a single extra penny. Unlimited is included in your package.

Do you see those boxes on the left side of each domain?

Click on the box that's associated with the website you want to host.

For you - it'll be easy. You probably have only one site right now.

Then you just want to click on the "Change Name servers" button.

It's right above your domain list. Here:

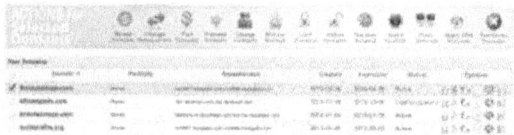

See it between "Renew Domains" and "Park Domains?"

Exactly.

Clicking on that button will take you to this page:

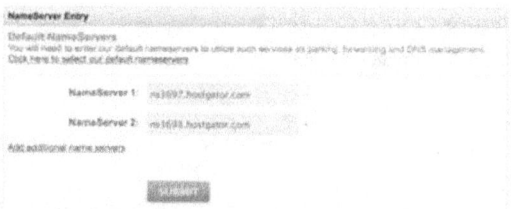

Just enter in your name servers, and everything will be smooth sailing.

Where the heck are your name servers?

Good question!

You can find your name servers in the Welcome Email from HostGator.

After you buy your web hosting, HostGator will send you this information instantly.

It'll look like this:

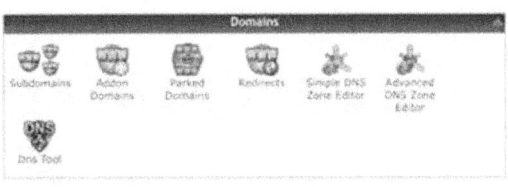

1st Nameserver: ns3697.hostgator.com
2nd Nameserver: ns3698.hostgator.com
Server IP: 184.173.250.156

See how those name servers match up with my NameSilo account.

That's how I connect the two services together.

There's just one more step, and then we'll start our new Wordpress site.

We need to add the domain to our HostGator C-Panel.

This is easy.

In your control panel, scroll down to the "Domains" section.

You want to click on "Add-On Domains"

Right here:

Click on that Add-on button.

Remember, you have to scroll down to find this section. If you don't see it, then you're either:

    1. Not in your c-panel

    2. Not scrolled down the page

The important part is that you enter the domain you just registered.

It'll look like this:

And there you have it.

A domain that's 100% connected to your hosting.

What's next?

Click on the "Get Started with Wordpress" button at the top of your HostGator C-Panel

Looks like this:

Follow a few easy steps, and you'll have a Wordpress site you can call your own.

That's it.

Congratulations!!! You have a website!

Pick a Passion with a Commercial Audience

Sounds like we're slipping into the hobby category here, but having a passionate interest in your blog are paramount to your success.

If you don't like your topic, you won't last for the long term.

You can fake an interest for a post or two. Maybe even a dozen.

To create a lucrative blog, you need years of posting the goods. With something that disinterests you, the content will burn out. Either altogether, or the apathy towards the subject will show in your writing.

Pick something that you like writing about.

Myself, for example, could ramble about "blogging" or "making money online" for days. I wouldn't stop, even if I became a billionaire tomorrow. It's what I enjoy doing.

Don't think of it as something you "could do," instead think of what you "have to do."

What about the Commercial Audience Part?

It would be nice if we could just stop at passion, right?

You'd be free to write about your favourite bag of Doritos, or the tasty Vietnamese restaurant down the road.

Blogging for money doesn't work that way. Where there's a passion, money often follows. But that's not always the case.

Some topics don't make bloggers enough sales to be worthwhile.

There are only really two things we need to worry about here:

1. Is the Audience Big Enough?

2. Does the Audience spend money?

Many will argue with me here, and say you also need to check the competition.

Logic being that if a topic like "make money online" is too competitive, you won't be able to muster enough attention to your blog.

I disagree. If a market has lots of competition, it's usually because there's money to be made.

You can get traffic in a competitive market. It will be harder, but worth it in the end.

For this, I like to lean on the wisdom of the former **Richest Man in the World.**

"In Business, I look for economic castles protected by unbreachable moats."

- Warren Buffet

If you're in a competitive marketplace, you just need to build a castle.

When you do that, you'll have a business that's sustainable and profitable.

Is your Passion Big Enough?

My advice would be, if you have to question it -- probably not.

The bloggers that make the big bucks are mostly in these industries:

- Make money online
- Health
- Fitness
- Finance
- Stock Market
- Fashion
- Celebrities
- Food
- Gaming(?)

That's a start.

You can probably find a half dozen more that are big enough to justify blogging for money.

What about smaller niches?

Here's the thing...

You absolutely could dominate a small niche. It would take some elbow grease, some time and some dedication to your niche audience. Even then, it would not be a guaranteed earner for you.

Let's say that you're interested in bowling. You could become one of the "bowling guys" in blogging. And yes, you would make a nice "side income."

However, it would actually be more difficult to make full-time income with bowling than it would in the fitness industry. Even though it's easier to become a bigger player in the bowling industry.

That make sense?

In the big industries, you can feast more on a much smaller sliver of the pie. If you pick a small blogging niche, you could eat the whole damn pie, and still be left hungry for more.

So find the middle ground that works for you.

I picked "make money online" when I started because it was the best financial choice. It also, fortunately for me, turned into a major passion of mine.

Your Blogging Purpose to the Reader

Your goal is probably a financial one.

When I started, my goal was to make my first $1 online.

Then my next goal was to reach $100/month. And the numbers continued to rise, until at the point of writing this, I make around $10,000 every month.

But **FORGET ALL THAT!**

Nobody cares about _your_ goal.

The reader wants to know what's in it for them.

You need a *Blogging Purpose*

This is a little tricky, because you don't want to just look like everyone else.

That's boring, and it's not going to build you a readership.

Instead, you want to stand out from the pack. You do this by having a USP (unique selling point).

A *Unique Selling Point* is the reason why a reader picks you.

For example, Pizza Hut is famous for selling a stuffed crust pizza. Cheese addicts will often select Pizza Hut because their _stuffed crust_ has captured their main interest.

In this case, we're talking about the Pizza Restaurant industry. Pizza Hut is the business, and a stuffed crust is their unique selling point.

Does that make sense?

The Three USP's on My Blog

I'll use my blog as an example.

On BrendanMace.com, there are three things I use to distinguish my brand from the pack.

    1. There's a mugshot of my face on the home page.

    2. I talk about travelling -- a lot.

    3. I'm transparent about pretty much everything.

For a little context, my blog is about "making money online"

That should help a little. It's not about finding something that's original to everything on the Internet. You'd expect a travel blog to talk about travelling, for instance.

A USP has to do with your particular industry. A good USP differentiates your blog from your competitors, and builds you readership.

A typical "make money online" blog is horrendous (in my opinion).

They usually have banner ads on the side, in the header of the blog, and even scattered throughout the post-copy.

Jamming ads is attractive because you can make some quick cash from an occasional sale.

You can make 10-20X more, however, by using the same "ad space" to sell yourself instead.

The mugshot of my face is different. It *intentionally* makes readers feel like they are reading from a real person. Of course, most blogs have a human writer involved. But it's easy to forget that, when half the page is packed with offers.

This is what I do, here:

Very simple, but stands out.

What could you do to make your blog more personal?

Simple little touches that add your personality go a long way. Your business is about developing connections with your readers. Do that -- and making cash will be easy.

The Travelling Rambles -- Why?

Another USP on **BrendanMace.com** is the constant 'travel talk.

Why?

My blog is about "**making money online.**" It may seem like a giant waste of words to focus on something that doesn't make money online, but it gives me a unique selling point.

There are loads of bloggers that brag about their numbers. Showing statistics about the amount of visitors they get per month, and how much net profit they make while sleeping in their mansions. And heck, I do some of this too (minus the mansion). But not many "make money online" bloggers talk about travelling.

To me, travelling is more down to earth. It's something many every-day guy or gal wants to do, but usually has a reason not to.

You may be thinking at this point, "I don't want to travel. I could care less about anything outside my basement."

And to that, I would say, "are you out of your fucking mind?"

Just kidding. Sort of...

The point I actually want to make is that you shouldn't try and please everyone. It's impossible, and you're more likely to be left with nobody.

The much better option is to build a tribe. To stand out, and grow a group of readers that are obsessed with your USP(s).

Full Transparency USP -- Industry specific

The last of my three USP's is transparency.

This would not be unique in other industries, like fitness or gaming.

When it comes to "make money online," however, most bloggers don't freely talk about their income sources, which is weird.

Keeping your hand hidden is the norm for Internet marketing.

For the clever bloggers out there, this unusual behavior is a welcome opportunity.

Any industry with lopsided norms is ripe for a **pattern interrupt.**

A "pattern interrupt" is an attention tsunami. Not everyone is going to like your interruption, but almost everyone will notice it.

Matthew Woodward -- A blogging Interrupter

Matthew Woodward has one of the coolest blogs in marketing.

His site clears 6-figures per year, and packs a blogging punch of awesomeness.

Matthew's most famous for his SEO (search engine optimization) ability. Which in layman's terms means his aptitude for ranking websites in search engines like Google.

When he started his blog, the blogging purpose was a "no back link experiment." Which means that he intended to demonstrate how to rank a website without building any backlinks.

The pattern for "website rankers" was to abuse backlinks. A typical blogger in that space would have experiments about how a certain 'link' affects a site's rankings.

It was unusual, for Matthew, to create an SEO focused blog that intentionally avoids backlinks.

That's like a world-class chef claiming he can make you a delicious meal without any food.

He did it, though. And his blog thrived because he chose to do something different.

How Do You Add a USP to Your Blog?

1. Brainstorm the norms in your market

2. Brainstorm what you could do differently

3. Pick at least one USP, and brand the crap out of it

Just be careful. Don't be different for the sake of difference.

Nobody is showing their genitals while blogging about mashed potatoes.

Sometimes nobody is doing something for a good reason.

Use your common sense to decide whether _your difference_, will give your blog the right purpose to move forward.

Your Site's Design and Layout

First of all, you need a logo.

Without one, you will not build a brand. And you will not look different.

My favourite spot for logo designs is a site called Fiverr.com

This site hosts a marketplace of freelancers that are willing to do small tasks for $5.

You can get anything from written articles to a drunken impersonation of Marilyn Monroe singing Happy Birthday. Lots of stuff. And everything is on the cheap.

If you're not careful, you can drop over $100 on random Fiverr gigs, though.

Cheap over time can really add up.

Here's my site's logo:

Simple, classy and gets my USP across.

My blog is about building a laptop business from a beach.

This logo captures that message, and it's not obnoxious about it.

Where did I get this awesome logo?

... You guessed it. On Fiverr.com for five buckaroos.

Here's the seller I bought from:

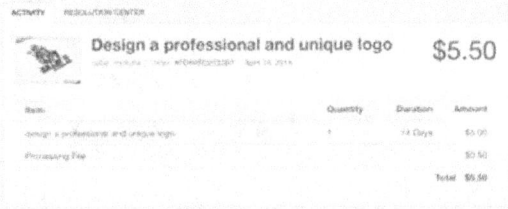

Awesome deal!

There's a bunch of logo designers on Fiverr.

Check it out, and save yourself the hassle of designing it yourself.

Using a Wordpress Theme to Shortcut the Look and Feel

In the past, if you wanted a "cool" looking blog, you'd either need professional web-designer skills, or you'd need to dish out thousands of dollars to have the design done for you.

That sucks.

Now you can get a professional blog design for less than 100 bucks. And I still see blog owners bitch and complain about dropping a little cash on a quality Wordpress theme.

That's a whole bowl of shortsightedness. These "Negative Nancy's" plan on making $1k+/month from their blog, but they can't drop $100 to get the right 'look and feel' for their website.

There are many bloggers that have split tested different designs and layouts. The income difference from one to the next is often massive.

Trust me, getting a quality look is one of the best investments in the business.

The Wordpress Themes I Recommend

You really cannot go wrong with **StudioPress Themes**.

This company has put together a smorgasbord of various Wordpress themes, so that you can find the exact one that fits your blogging needs.

The theme used on BrendanMace.com is called MagazinePro

You can see it here:

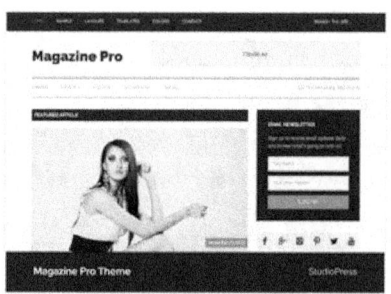

It cost me $97, which may seem expensive to some. In the grand scheme of things, less than $100 on a serious business is a bargain.

Side Note: Blogging for money is a business -- not a hobby. If you opened a business on Main Street, think of all the expenses you would pay.

You'd owe rent, utilities, cost of goods, worker salaries, etc.

Just because your expenses with an online business are typically lower, that does not mean you should avoid investing at all costs.

When you have an opportunity to drop a little money to improve your business a lot -- take that opportunity.

What to Write in Your Blog Posts

The "work" involved in blogging is the content creation.

Sure, once you have a steady online income stream, you'll be able to afford outsourcing some of this content creation, if you want to.

Until then, you will need to write this stuff yourself.

Your blogging livelihood depends on the posts you write. Understandably, this is an important problem that you will have to solve.

My recommendation is to do some keyword research.

The key here is to find out what people are searching for on Google.

The easiest and cheapest way to get (some) keyword information is to go direct to the source.

With the first easy keyword strategy, open up Google.com on your browser, and start typing in industry related words.

What we're looking for here is the "auto generated keyword suggestions."

These suggestions tell us what people are commonly looking for.

An example here shows the a simple search of "blogging f"

Right away, we can see that "blogging for beginners" and for 'money' are two very popular options.

If we were blogging on the topic "make money blogging" these would be great keywords to target.

The problem here is that blogging relies on many blog posts over time. If we just wanted a keyword or two, this autocomplete strategy would work.

However, we need more, so we need a more expansive tool.

My favourite tool for getting keywords quick and easy is LongTailPro.

You can find my **full review of it here**.

Side Note: The last couple sections both recommend spending a little money to shortcut your blogging. I promise you there is not much left to buy. However, these little investments are worth your while.

How to Get Traffic to Your Blog

As proved by Matthew's blog, you're better off ignoring backlinks.

You may have never heard about the benefits of backlinks before. If that's the case, consider yourself lucky. The strategy of abusing backlinks for rankings is not realistic anymore.

The better option is to use <u>high quality content,</u> "*in the right way*" to get traffic.

That 'right way' part will be discussed in a moment.

The only way people are going to see your blog, is if you show it to them.

What is the Right Way to Promote Your Blog?

We know that backlinks aren't going to work, and playing the waiting game is futile.

The best option is to get our content in front of an audience.

There are a few ways to do that, but in this guide, I'm going to feature my favourite three.

The Biggest Myth of Blog Traffic

In the blogging sphere, there's an annoying little myth, which discourages actual progress.

This myth is that great content is enough.

Let me explain why this is untrue with an analogy.

One of my favourite movies from the 80's was **Field of Dreams**.

Just a couple weeks ago, I watched it with my girlfriend, and despite her dislike of baseball, she still thought it was a great flick.

It's often misquoted with "Build it and They Will Come"

When in actuality, it was "<u>Build it and He Will Come</u>"

While it was a feel good moment in the movie, if you treat your blog this way, you are going to get hosed.

In other words, you'll never see good traffic or Google rankings.

This is something most people don't realize. They expect people to come.

The Fantasy Unravels

There's this notion that:

If you build it, they will come.

This appeals to us because it seems like a fair deal.

You provide value and you're rewarded with TRAFFIC.

Not true!

The reality is that it's not what you write that matters...

It's how you **_MARKET_** what you write.

You could have the best-written content in the world. It does not matter.

Who's going to see it?

How to Market Your Crap?

This is a BIG topic.

I mean *big* in more ways than one.

Firstly, it's big in terms of importance.

Traffic is the oxygen of your business.

Without it - your site will die.

Secondly, it's discussed a lot.

Which leads to information overload. And a myriad of frustrated marketers.

There are many strategies for **getting traffic to your blog.**

The most popular two are breadcrumbs and the skyscraper technique.

In this post, we'll be looking at **my results** from the latter.

What is the Skyscraper Technique?

The concept is simple.

1. Find a blog post with TONS of social shares. Let's call this **Post X.**

2. Create something better than **Post X**. Make it longer, more visual, and more exceptional.

3. Contact the people that shared **Post X**, and show them *YOUR* stuff.

Easy enough, right?

This leads us to a couple crucial questions.

- Where do we find these posts?
- Where do we find these sharers?

There's ONE tool that does both of these for you.

BuzzSumo (no affiliation) is a search engine that scrapes the amount of social sharers for any topic of your choice.

Here's a look for the BuzzSumo search: How to Make Money on YouTube

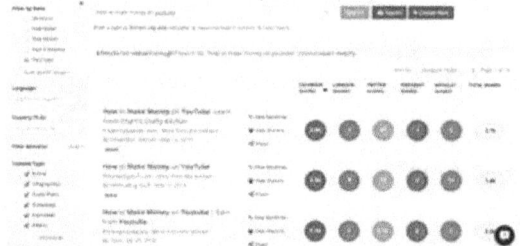

When you type in any search, BuzzSumo reveals what content has the most shares.

But wait...

It gets even better than that.

Clicking on **"View Sharers,"** actually shows **_WHO_** shared it.

As seen here:

After clicking on "View Sharers"

...BuzzSumo will provide you with a list of the people that shared that piece of content.

Pretty cool, right?

But what the heck can I do with that?

Welcome to the Skyscraper Method

Now we can take our list of sharers, and contact them directly.

There are a number of ways to do this.

We can:

1. Tag them in a Tweet

2. Email them from their website

3. Call them on the phone

The most common way is **option #2**

It also happens to be quite easy to do.

We go to their website, and then we find their "contact us" page.

Not all websites have these - but the good one's will.

Then we send them a message.

Here's where it ***gets a little dicey...***

When you contact potential sharers of your blog, you have a couple ways to go.

You could bluntly ask them to share your stuff. This will have a reasonably high success rate.

BUT it will also piss off a bunch of future contacts.

I do NOT recommend this!

The better option is to just let them know about your content.

Some marketers would consider this quite passive. And in general, it's the kind of behaviour that's frowned upon in **Make Money Online.**

It stands out, though. In a good way.

Instead of being pushy, you're kindly sharing a good post with them.

We already know these contacts are willing to share stuff. That's how we found them.

With just a little nudge, we can get them to share OUR stuff.

The whole idea here is that you are finding the right people.

And showing them something you know they'll be interested in.

Now, let's look at an example...

I created a long 4,000+ post on <u>How to Grow a YouTube Channel.</u>

This post was exceptional.

It covered the whole process of how to get YouTube subscribers, and even shared a couple lesser-known tricks to steal some easy traffic. Highly recommended post.

So I wanted to test the ***Skyscraper Technique*** on this post to see what kind of results I could get with it.

So I went into my copy of BuzzSumo, and search for YouTube Marketing.

My search found some really good stuff.

Take a look:

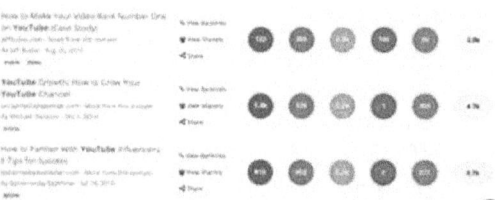

So I completed the Skyscraper Technique as discussed.

I clicked on "View Sharers"

And I started contacting these sharers one by one.

It was tedious.

I hated it.

But I started getting some results.

If you know anything about me, though, you'll know that I HATE WORK!

Seriously.

This <u>whole blog</u> and <u>YouTube channel</u> started because I didn't want a day job.

Boring tasks are the bane of my existence.

And they should be for you, too.

So I found a guy on FaceBook willing to complete these tasks for $5/hour.

Can you imagine that?

ONLY FIVE BUCKS

... FOR A FULL HOUR!!

Turns out when you find someone that lives in a county like, Thailand or the Philippines, they are very likely to work for cheap. Their cost of living is a lot lower, and consequently need a lot less money to pay their bills.

Side note: I'm off to Thailand on February 2nd.

One of the BEST advantages of the laptop lifestyle!

Anyways, so I purchased 5 hours from this dude in total.

Here's our first messages back-and-forth:

I gave him $25, and he contacted these sharers for 5 hours.

Later in this post, I'm going to reveal the results.

I also created a video, detailing the task.

This is not mandatory, but it made it easier for me to explain.

If this video would help you get someone to do this task, feel free to direct them to the below video:

Warning: I'm really sick in this video, and it's far from a good production.

But, it outlines what's expected for this task, if you plan to outsource like I did.

In my opinion, it's worthwhile to outsource any task that's boring.

Especially when people will do it of for only $5.

Moving On:

Immediately after starting this task. I started receiving email replies from a handful of sharers.

Pretty exciting stuff.

Some of the messages were from people that were downright PISSED.

Here's one:

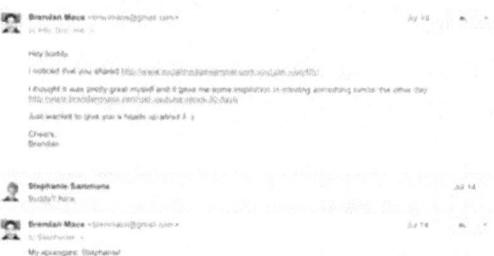

My preference is to ALWAYS include someone's name. Instead of a term like: "buddy"

Unfortunately, Stephanie's website didn't provide her name.

Or, BuzzSumo was unable to properly scraper name information.

This stuff happens.

Don't let it ruin your day.

There was, of course, also a bunch of positive responses to my message.

Here's one of them:

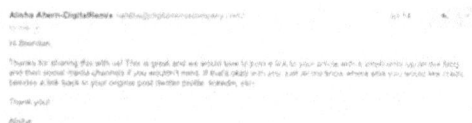

This message led to a very pleasant conversation. Both of us were able to help each other out in very constructive ways.

Booyah!

At the end of the day - how were the results?

The results were decent.

This turned out to be a worthwhile investment of $25.

But it was not a silver bullet.

There are two things that we care about the most here:

    1. How many shares did I get?

2. How much money did I make?

How many shares?

I was actually hoping for more...

I ended up with these results:

- 44 Twitter shares

- 42 FaceBook shares

- 10 Google Plus Shares

For a total of 96 shares.

Not bad.

How much money did I make?

From this post launching, I can attribute TWO affiliate sales for $42 a pop.

That works out to be $84 in gross revenue from this method.

Minus $25 for outsourcing costs.

We're looking at a ***profit of $59***

Not massive. But that's free money.

I paid someone else to do the work.

And I collected the affiliate commissions.

Would I recommend this strategy?

100% I would.

As mentioned before, this is not a silver bullet.

It will not get you rich.

However, it's a good way to make some easy money while building some nice social shares at the same time.

Of course, your content needs to be very good to get these results.

My post on **Growing a YouTube Channel** was top notch.

Don't expect to throw up a junky 500-word article, and get similar results.

The people you are contacting are willing to share, but ONLY if its good stuff.

Other Way to Get Extra Traffic

The Skyscraper Method and Guest Posting are both great ways to get traffic.

They do require a lot of work, though.

An easier way to get traffic is what I like to call the "Infiltrator Method"

The idea is simple

1. Find out where your audience hangs out

2. Add value to the conversation(s)

3. Siphon back to your blog

The best way to find your audience is to use a tagging based system.

There's a free tool called **Google Alerts,** where you'll be sent a "keyword based" notification anytime Google discovers new content that is created in your subject area.

This is a 100% free way to get more traffic.

All you need to do is monitor the notifications, and then siphon traffic back from the source Google finds.

There's a bit of a trick here, though.

It's not enough to go to these publications, and shamelessly drop your link back to your blog.

Any site with reasonable quality control will delete your link. Meaning that only the lower quality sites will even let you post that kind of garbage.

The better way to do this is to **provide value first**. Then when you drop your link, the site owner will recognize that your contribution is not entirely selfish. It's a win-win to keep you there.

It's even okay to have a "copy + paste" message written up on a topic area. And in fact, that's probably the most effective way to do it.

For example, if I use a Google Alerts for "keyword research," I have a template message already created on how to get the best results with keywords. At the end of this template message, I let people know that if they want more information, they can visit my blog for more details.

Instead of re-writing this message every time, I can use it *__any time__* that Google has a notification for "keyword research."

I may have to edit it a tiny bit to personalize it to the particular post. But overall, this copy and paste system will save me a lot of time.

Finding a Forum to Add Value

Another great opportunity is to Google search for forums in your area.

When I Google search "make money online" forums, right away I see two results:

Making Money - BlackHatWorld
www.blackhatworld.com/blackhat-seo/111-making-money/ ▾
Forum: Making Money ... Discuss all CryptoCurrencies / coins and their use within the
Making Money Niche. ... Discuss the future of Making Money Online here.

make money online - Warrior Forum - The #1 Digital Marketin...
www.warriorforum.com/tags/make%20money%20online.html ▾
3 days ago - coaching, freedom, make money, make money online, money Go to first
new post CLOSING - 30 Days To Freedom Challenge.. Watch LIVE As I ...

BlackHatWorld and WarriorForum are both goldmines of potential blog readers.

Not only can you get a lot of visitors back to your blog. The traffic is generally very response.

After all, think about it. The reason why people clicked over to your site is because they like what you had to say.

This is going to be like random Google traffic that stumbles on your site.

It's going to be laser-targeted visitors that already position you as an expert.

Your user metrics for "time on site" will go through the roof. Which will indirectly help your Google rankings as well.

Talk about a powerful traffic strategy.

All you need for "Forum Marketing" is to have a good signature.

Here's mine:

FREE Keyword Research Tutorial "REVEALS" 36 THOUSAND Keywords in ONLY 5 Minutes
>>> Adsense vs Amazon vs Clickbank - See Who Wins! (my blog) <<<
>>> My YouTube Channel - Loads of FREE Videos <<<

Everything is in **BOLD TEXT** and encourages people to click over.

The more value you add in the forum, the more likely people will visit your site.

If you're seen as an expert on the forum -- even better.

Visitors will be flocking to your site, ready to give you their well-earned attention.

Building a List from Blog Readers

In the next chapter, I'll be covering list building in even more depth. Until then, this chapter will introduce you to the power of emails.

If you don't build a list, you're leaving <u>most</u> of the money on the table.

Notice, I'm saying "most" here -- that's true.

Think about it, if you get one Google visitor, you probably have a chance to make *only one sale on that day*.

If you capture a subscriber, you can keep a loyal follower for life.

... That's ***365 emails per year*** (at a rate of one per day) and a load of extra blog visits and affiliate sales.

It's pretty clear. Capturing the lead is your number one monetization strategy.

The Best Way to Convert Visitors into Subscribers

Put Email Form(s) directly on Your Site

There are lots of vacant places on your blog for an email form.

I have a few places that I recommend the most:

- On your sidebar

- On your blog header

- Before your content

- In the content

- Pop Up for Visitor Departures

You can really get creative here. If you're really a stickler for maximizing conversion rates, you could boost up your numbers by having specific forms for each specific post.

For example, a blog post about "list building" could have an email form that promises an "Email Marketing Cheat Sheet" bonus. In order to get that cheat sheet, visitors would need to subscribe to the specific web-form on that one specific blog post.

It would take a bit of extra work, but the extra opt-ins may be worth your while. I'll be honest here and say I don't do this. It takes a good amount of time, and I'd rather focus on other areas of my business.

For simplicity sake, my favourites for ***on-blog*** email forms are **the sidebar**, the **pop up** and **before the content**.

My blog doesn't actually have a sidebar form. Not because it's a bad idea, I simply went in another direction.

The **Pop Up,** however, results in the largest portion of my new subscribers.

I enthusiastically encourage you to add this to your blog.

Won't a pop up bother my visitors?

Great question.

Some people will take this the wrong way -- that's an unavoidable reality for pretty much anything you create.

But really, why should anyone care?

The **Pop Up** that I use is easily closed able, which is important to me, and makes the brief pop up interruption as short as a half taken breath.

In fact, it doesn't in any way prevent visitors from leaving my site.

It activates when a visitor indicates they are about to leave, and encourages visitors to join my blog mailing list. If a visitor still decides they want to leave without subscribing, this offer in no way prevents them from doing so.

Any person that complains about a non-obstructing pop up needs to chill.

And besides, they're leaving anyways.

This is your last chance at gaining a long-term visitor to your blog. Any subscribers are a huge bonus that will provide easy traffic for any future posts.

Here's a look at my pop up:

Check out my blog, and you can see this pop up in real time.

The other place "on my blog" that collects leads on autopilot is the before content form.

This next form is a little more obstructing.

In this case, visitors see the form before they see any of your content.

To some people, this is really off-putting. Because before you even add any value, you're already asking for a favour.

While this does get subscribers, I can understand why this would prompt some people to leave your site earlier.

For that reason, I only have this form on my home page.

That way, it doesn't distract from my blog content in any significant way. And most people that really enjoy my blog content will visit the home page and see my form.

You can see my before content form here:

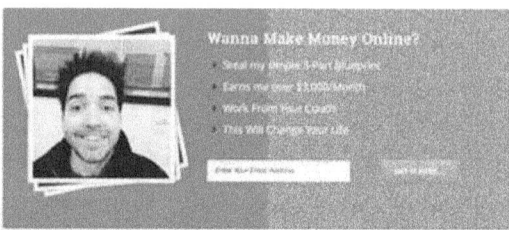

These two "on-site" forms roll in some free subscribers.

The crucial concept in this section is that blog followers via email are what separate full-time bloggers from struggling "wantrapreneurs."

A good blogger finds a way to build a returning audience.

The easiest way to do that is with an email list.

What Emails Should You Send to New Subscribers?

Your best option is to create an email series.

The service I use is **Aweber**

You can get a <u>**30 day free trial of Aweber right here.**</u>

In your free trial of Aweber, you need to click on the "Create a Message button"

You can see this green button on the right side of your account.

Here's a look at mine:

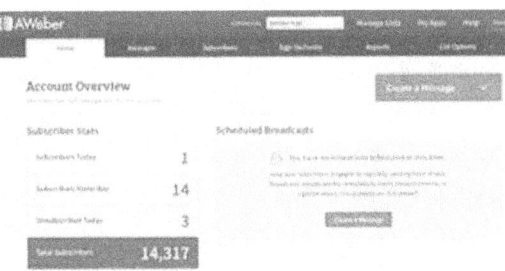

You'll then be taking to an editor.

This looks just like Microsoft Word, or whatever word processor that you're used to.

Basically, you create your emails, and then save them when you're done.

I recommend creating at least 20 emails to start, and then build over time.

Actually, my email series is over 240+ messages.

It didn't get that way overnight; I gradually keep adding more emails over time.

Don't worry, though. Emails are not like blog posts. They don't have to be long.

Just a simple, to the point message to your subscribers.

The best email conversions happen when you create personal emails. Subscribers feel like you are talking directly to them, and not like you're just blasting out to thousands of people at once.

Keep that in mind while you write your email series.

Here's a look at my first five messages in the series:

1. Booyah! YOU are now subscribed to Brendan Mace

2. Create Your Own $867.26/month Niche Site

3. Crazy NEW Keyword Method - 100% Awesome

4. Easy Steps to Unlimited Traffic on Autopilot

5. Create a Profitable Niche Site in 20 Minutes or Less

Not only will email get more visitors to your blog, it will also make you sales as well.

The emails that I write serve a number of different purposes.

1-- My Coaching program

My emails often tell people about my coaching services.

In **my coaching program** I share absolutely everything I know about "making money online" and we set everything up together step-by-step.

This allows me to help many followers achieve their goals, and many actually quit their jobs.

My business only takes about 15 minutes per day to maintain, and I make enough to pay all my bills.

2-- Blog/Video Tutorials

In these emails, I direct traffic to my online tutorials. This builds a relationship with my list, gets traffic to my blog, and also helps people learn new marketing skills.

This essentially leverages the valuable content you create on your blog, and serves it up to an active and engaged audience.

3-- Affiliate Promotions

When I find a product worth recommending, I'll send an email to my subscribers letting them know about it.

These emails are delicate. You do not want to promote garbage. That will ruin your reputation faster than obnoxiously farting on a first date.

I wait for products that I actually use myself before sharing with my subscribers.

This works the same for blog or email.

Two Simple Steps:

>   1. Find good products

>   2. Promote them

Easy cash, and useful to many.

4-- Engagement Driven Emails

These are my personal favourite of the emails I send.

Their purpose is simple -- to get engagement.

An example email subject line I use is "***How Can I Help You?***"

In this email, I'm asking subscribers to contact me with whatever they need help with.

Many subscribers do take me up on this, and I fortunately get to work with many of my followers.

Some refuse to do this. After all, it takes some "*real work*" to engage directly with your subscribers.

In my opinion, it's an exceptional use of your time.

An average engagement response takes me 60 seconds or less. In most cases subscribers are asking a specific question that really only takes one or two paragraphs to answer.

In that 60 second or less timespan, I have usually created a loyal follower for life.

The subscribers I answer will see my email more often, buy more products from my recommendations, and definitely follow my blog more closely.

This is one relatively untapped area with a goldmine of value.

Do not underestimate the power of helping people directly.

Why Site Speed Matters

One of the biggest mistakes people make is ignoring site speed.

There are two problems with having low speed.

1. It Creates a bad user experience

2. Google will hate you for it

In the mess of writing posts and promoting content, it sometimes gets forgotten to look at the overall experience.

Any user that visits a slow website is more likely to bounce, and a lot less likely to buy.

Google's disdain for slow loading times is getting even more intense.

And it makes sense for this search behemoth to care so much. Having a bad user experience is unprofessional. It may seem unfair for Google to penalize so harshly, but they are usually just looking for accurate indicators about a site's quality.

You'll get fewer visitors to a slow site, and the people you get are less likely to stay as long.

The good news is that site speed is easy to improve.

The Main Problems that Ruin Your Site Speed -- And what to do about it

A couple years ago, I had no idea how the Internet worked.

While on vacation in Cuba, I noticed that my blog was running way slower.

My first reaction was that Cuba must have terrible Internet speed.

The confusion, though, was that websites like **Google** and **FaceBook** maintained a high-speed connection.

Why Would My Blog Get the Short End of the Stick?

And then I found out.

When visiting my blog, the information from my blog's server location has to virtually travel to the location of my Internet connection.

In simpler talk, if my blog is set up in Seattle, USA, and someone opens it elsewhere, the information has to travel all the way from Seattle to that visitor's location.

That means that any person close to my hosting server will get the fastest site speeds, but most international visitors will have a much slower experience.

The easy fix for this is to use a CDN.

What is a Content Delivery Network?

A CDN is a network of servers that distributes your content delivery around the globe.

Each visitor is sent your site's information from the country on the CDN that's the closest to his or her location.

This means that regardless of whether a visitor is in South East Asia, Europe, Cuba, etc., your site will consistently deliver a faster site speed.

A good option for this is called MaxCDN (no affiliation)

This small change will dramatically improve your blog's speed for visitors around the world.

Another Important Blog Decision for Site Speed

You must know that you need a hosting service.

This will affect the site speed.

My best recommendation is to use **HostGator for budget hosting.**

There are very expensive hosting providers that deliver the fastest site speeds. The one I'm using for BrendanMace.com costs me $50/month. That's something you'll want to add as your blog grows past 10,000 visitors per month.

Until then, most hosting services are between $4-10/month.

HostGator is a very reasonable price. It costs about $5/month for the Baby Plan.

If you use the coupon code **"get25offyourbill"** you'll get an additional 25% discount off your hosting order.

Benefits of Blogging for Money

Every month, I post my business results on my blog.

I call these income reports.

As of right now, I'm making around **$10,000 per month.**

The even better news is that my business really only takes about 15 minutes per day to maintain.

That means that on a low effort month, I would spend about *7.5 hours* working.

During that month, I would still make $10,000.

Which means that my income rate is approximately **$1,333.33/hour**.

That's the number after taking my income and dividing it by hours worked.

What to Do with All that Time?

Tim Ferris calls this the New Rich.

The idea being that time is an asset that's at least as valuable as money.

Under this philosophy, even a millionaire could be "time-poor," if a job prevents him from living his life.

It's not just about making money.

It's also about building an income stream that doesn't enslave your precious time.

To become a member of the new rich, you must build passive income.

When you do that, you'll win back your life.

What I do with My Time

In the last eight months I've traveled to:

- The Okanagan

- Vancouver

- Las Vegas

- Cuba

- Medellin

- San Andreas Island

- Panama City

- Thailand

- Cambodia

- Vietnam

Here's a view shot of the beach at Koh Tao:

To me, travelling is what keeps me sane.

It's not just about making the money that's important. It's what I do with my time that matters the most.

There are a lot people that say, "Money doesn't buy happiness"

Which is a debatable statement. You have both sides of the coin here. In my opinion, it's shortsighted to think money can't affect your life.

The truth is that money may not buy happiness, but poverty can buy a whole lot of misery.

The reason for making money blogging is to give you freedom.

We all have our reasons for wanting this.

For me, I want to be laying on a beach on my terms. And work only when I want to.

You know what the crazy thing is?

Travelling the world is not that expensive.

When you trade dollars for pesos, your money will go a lot further.

Nomadic Matt is a travel blogger.

He also wrote a book titled "How to Travel the World on $50 per Day"

That's just $1,500 per month. And that's an average of every country in the whole freaking world. You could live even cheaper if you slumber onto a beach area in South East Asia.

Do you need to travel?

Absolutely not.

But find something worth doing with your time.

For some of us, that means more time to spend with the family.

For others, that might just mean a little more down time for television and movies. Don't feel guilty about that. Many of us have been working too hard for too many years.

It's time to win your life back.

Start blogging!

Chapter 6 – List Building

A lot of people talk about how to make money with lists, but not many people actually go into any detail.

In this chapter, I'm going to take you behind the scenes of my $5,000 a month business that takes me around 20 minutes per day to maintain.

On top of that, I'm going to share my personal 110+ email autoresponder sequence with you so you can learn how to do the same.

At the end of this tutorial you will have learned how to create a list building funnel that brings in new profit and leads every single day.

What You Will Learn

- My 2 step list building formula

- How to create your own list building business

- How to build an auto responder sales funnel

- How to buy traffic & make instant money

- How to build & maintain a relationship with your list automatically

This is the story of how I work less than <u>four hours per week</u>, but still managed to build 40K+ leads in *less than a year* on a shoe string budget.

Having over 40,000 email subscribers at your fingertips means daily affiliate commissions and free traffic anywhere you want.

More importantly though, it's easy, cheaper than you think and only takes about 20 mins per day to maintain.

 By working faithfully eight hours a day you may eventually get to be boss and work twelve hours a day.

Imagine waking up on **YOUR** terms. No early commute in traffic. Waiting in your car, behind a line of exhaust-filled vehicles. Desperately needing a shot of espresso to keep yourself awake just long enough to endure 8 full hours of your employer's BS.

That's a scary story, that unfortunately, relates to wayyyyy too many of us. Your life can be different. Mine is. I escaped. Let me tell ya how...

==> PASSIVE INCOME <==

The secret sauce to building virtual assets with <u>RESIDUAL</u> income is creating a repeatable business model.

That's why you're reading this book!

"Why hustle for hours to make the same income, when you can almost as easily create something with recurring profits? Once they're up and running, it can rake in profits <u>FOREVER</u>.

Just set it and forget it!"

– Ron Popeil, Founder of RONCO – Over $1 billion in revenue

Set what??

...What the F#$K is *"it?"*

In affiliate marketing terms, "it" could be a wide variety of things. Some of which include: niche sites, Facebook Pages, T-shirt campaigns, YouTube channels, Kindle books, arbitrage and so on...

In this post, we're building a *virtual sales funnel*.

Once set up, this funnel will:

- Provide value

- Collect leads

- Generate sales

And the best part, building an email list is creating a virtual property that can net you MUCH MORE than the J-O-B, for a LOT less work.

"[Luke] I can't believe it.

[Yoda] That is why you fail."

—Star Wars

Ok okay... Last quote, I promise. How could I resist Star Wars?

Anywho, this blog post is not your typical, press these buttons and watch as your bank account explodes with affiliate commissions.

NOPE... It ain't that easy.

That being said, if you break down this formula into it's separate parts, it won't be that hard either.

My "Rocket Science" Two-Step Formula:

- Step 1: Build a List

- Step 2: Promote Stuff

You don't need to create your own product. And you don't need to worry about specific details, like when to send and how many affiliate products to promote, etc.

Sure, there are guidelines to follow. But as long as you're building a list and notifying them about "cool stuff" as it comes out, you will make money with this...

The Ethical Bribe

The reality is that you're not going to have subscriber numbers like these overnight:

I knew that building a list was going to be a gradual process. What I didn't realize is that you can actually make a lot of money while you build your list. But more on that later...

We're starting at the beginning, which means **building your landing page.**

For those of us unfamiliar to the term "landing page" it literally just means a page on your site that is designed to collect email subscribers.

The way it works is simple, your task is to perform an ethical bribe.

An "ethical bribe" in marketing, is a promise of value in exchange for an email address.

- You get subscribers

- They get value

What Can You Give Away Of Value?

Chances are, especially if you're an active reader of Matt's blog, that you have internet marketing knowledge that would benefit other people.

Your freebie could be:

- a video

- an ebook

- a blog post

Just something that adds value. A lot of people get freaked out about this step. *That's unnecessary.* You don't need to giveaway a secret marketing method that only you know about.

As long as some people don't know (or have) your freebie and you're helping them reach their goals, your freebie is just fine.

Don't Want To Create Your Own Freebie?

You don't even have to... If you're determined to avoid this step, you can STILL be successful. Goes to show that there are MANY ways to make income with sales funnels.

One option is to embed an informative YouTube video on your blog and then send them to your blog for your freebie. You could even add your own affiliate links into your blog post and collect a little extra **BONUS** income from this strategy.

Another valid work-around is to purchase PLR (private label rights) products. What this means, is that someone took the time to create an entire product or freebie and then is selling the rights to brand this product as your own.

The real advantage of option 2 is that you get to position yourself as an authority. By slapping your name on a high quality PLR product, you appear like an expert in your field.

Even though you literally spent only a few minutes to add your name and branding to the packaging.

Here's a PLR catalog with a lot of top notch stuff: HQ Biz in a Box

Take a look at a couple examples...

Ex. 1 –List Building PLR Package

Ex. 2 – SEO Made Easy PLR Package

Pretty cool stuff, huh?

These PLR packages are completely DONE-FOR-YOU with sales pages, squeeze pages, free reports and follow up emails.

The point is, you have options:

 • Create your own freebie

- Steal someone else's (i.e. YouTube Video)

- Buy PLR and rebrand it

I have personally used all three options in separate funnels and they all get the job done. Pick you own plan of attack and let's move on to the bribing!!

Bribing Cold Traffic With Your Awesome Freebie?

Get your freebie and let's create a landing page that makes it desirable.

My freebie is a video series that I created on my Two Step Formula. Sound familiar? It's the exact strategy that I'm giving away in this post. You can see my video series here.

Two Step Formula:

- Step 1: Build List

- Step 2: Promote

My Freebie: Video Series on "Make Money Online"

Now we need to take this (or your) freebie and design a page that promises it in exchange for email addresses.

In marketing, this is called a squeeze page.

Here's the one I created for this freebie:

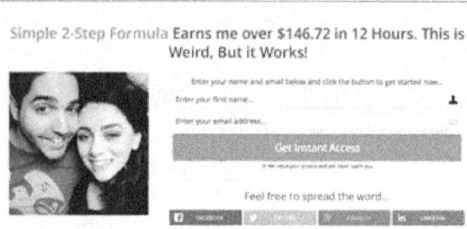

You'll notice a few things about this squeeze page, but let's break it down.

How to Get a 56% Conversion Rate

First thing…

My landing page is really simple. It has a headline, an image, some share buttons, and an opt-in box.

This simplicity is intentional. Simple squeeze pages convert way better. The more you add to squeeze pages, the lower they convert.

Most visitors from cold traffic have an attention span of 5 seconds or less. They're like goldfish. They visit your page, make a snap judgement and then move on.

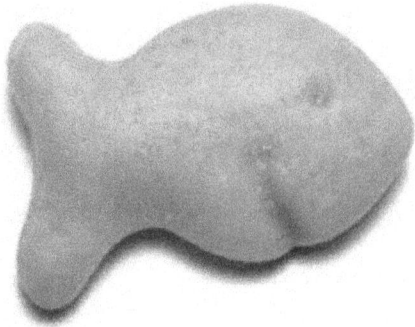

Hey, I'm not being judgemental. I'm a **goldfish** visitor, too. Other than Facebook, YouTube and a few others, I'll only invest a few seconds on your page before I decide whether to stay.

You need to grab visitor's attention and clearly give your proposition of value, but it all needs to be done in a matter of a few seconds. Tough task.

Less is more, but the less is still important. It needs to have curiosity.

Second thing...

A good squeeze page creates optimistic curiosity. It leaves a little to the imagination. Think of the squeeze page as the lingerie to the... well, you know...

In this squeeze page, I tell visitors about a mysterious "**Two-Step Formula**" that leads to near instant riches.

What 2-Step formula? Is it going to cost me anything?

... I don't tell them anything. That is, I'm not telling until they give me their email address.

Get it?

Curiosity is a h*** of a drug. It gets people in. They have to know, it's just human nature.

So to here's what you need for a successful squeeze page:

- Simple (clear to visitors within seconds)
- Proposition of value (you will make money with this)
- Curiosity (secret ingredient that significantly boosts opt-ins)

Overall, that squeeze page is averaging a **58.62%** Opt-in rate. The industry avg is around 30-40%... I'm not saying this to brag (well maybe just a little), but the main take away is that a good squeeze page is simple... BUT makes sure that every word counts.

How to Create A Winning Headline

The headline is the most important element on your squeeze page. It will make and break your conversion rate and in general, should be tested and tweaked many times.

But as a starting point, let's throw one together real quick.

When I was first learning how to create these, I was fortunate enough to stumble across an article from Eben Pagan that revealed a number of powerful headline formulas.

I'm going to share two of them with you now.

Headline Formula #1: The Quick n' Easy

This one combines three elements into a single headline and it works like this.

How to [insert benefit here] in [a short amount of time] with [very little work]

Example: How to Easily Get 150+ Email Subscribers in the Next 24 Hours

You'll notice that the example headline doesn't exactly match the order of the template. But that's really beside the point.

The key here is that your headline promises an exceptionally good result, in a quick amount of time with very little work.

It doesn't matter how you order it, as long as it includes all three elements.

Headline Formula #2: Your Problem, my Fix

This one's pretty simple. Explain what's going wrong and then hint at a solution.

Why [this typical method] is [not working]... and what to do...

Example: Why list building no longer works like it used to... and what to do about it

This one is meant to position yourself as the person with THE solution.

Everyone else is doing the same old thing and it's no longer working. Let me show you what does.

This headline can be really powerful and it's obvious why it works so well. Most subscribers are looking for that one secret or tool that will take them over the edge and finally make money online.

You're telling them that you have the answer.

Perfect!! We've covered headlines. Thanks Pagan.

Designing Your Squeeze Page

I'm going to be 100% transparent here... I've never designed a squeeze page from scratch, ever. Notta single one. Nada. Zilch.

And honestly, unless you are exceptionally skilled at graphic design and/or do-it-yourself projects, then you're way better off doing it the easy way.

Outsource it or get an awesome **head start**

My shortcut to creating *outrageously* high converting landing pages is WP Profit Builder.

It's a tool that does 95% of the design process for you. The ONLY thing you need to do is adjust the text. That's it.

The way Profit Builder works is simple. It's a WordPress Plugin that loads dozens of squeeze templates into your blog.

These templates are already top notch quality pages. So pretty much, everything is done-for-you.

Here are some examples:

Ex. 1 – High Converter

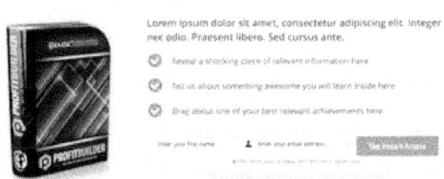

Ex. 2 – Bloom

Ex. 3 – Exotic

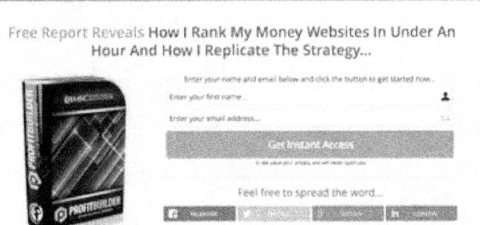

Last template look familiar to you?

It should! It's the same template I used to create my current squeeze page as shown above.

You'll notice that I did very little to change the template. Just clicked a couple buttons, uploaded a replacement photo and edited the text. All in – it took me about 5-6 minutes of work.

… And my current squeeze page regularly gets over 55% opt-in rates. As a point of reference, the industry average is around 30%.

Not too shabby for a few minutes of my time.

The good news is that you can do this, too. It may take you a bit longer than 5 minutes. But I'd bet within half an hour you could create a real good looking page.

You could also use LeadPages or something like OptimizePress if you already have them to create something similar.

The Instant Offer

In chapter 4, we swing on to step #2… Promote stuff!!

There's a real sweet spot here. We don't want to ONLY send promotions – that'll burn our list into bits.

We need to build at least some kind of good-will with our subscribers.

On the flip side, we can't only focus on providing value and neglect promotions. That's where we make the money.

So I'm going to tell you **EXACTLY** what I do to accomplish both.

But before all that, there's a little $$$ we need to make first.

And that's right after our visitor opts-in. We need a front-end offer.

Why The Front End Offer Is Critical?

You won't make any money unless you get traffic. In order to guarantee that some eyeballs actually see your landing page, you'll need to buy traffic yourself.

Sure, getting organic traffic with the whole "build it and they'll come" approach is a nice fantasy.

And yes, there are some cumbersome ways to get small trickles of free traffic to your squeeze. The reality though, is that if you want traffic – go to the traffic store and buy it!

BUT!!

Buying traffic is pretty darn expensive. And unless we have a larger sized budget, it won't take too long to burn through our advertising spend. The **BETTER** way is to include an offer **IMMEDIATELY** after visitors subscribe.

That way, we can easily pay for traffic and make money at the same time.

If we then reinvest our front-end sales on more traffic, it's not farfetched to have an UNLIMITED supply of visitors to our page.

It Works Like This

Money ==> Traffic ==> Subscribers + Front End Sales (money) ==> Traffic ==> Sales ==> Traffic ==> Sales ==> Traffic ==> Sales ==> Repeat.

… You'll notice that the process just repeats. Every time you buy more traffic, you get two things.

- Sales to reinvest on traffic

- New subscribers

The sales to reinvest on traffic help you in the short term. Without front-end sales, you cannot buy unlimited traffic.

You will eventually run out of money and will have to wait to make money from your subscribers.

The subscribers have a more **LONG TERM** value. These are real people that can/will open your emails for years to come if you do it right.

Building up your list is your primary goal. You do that by investing on traffic. You can only have an unlimited supply of traffic if you make money immediately after opt-in.

What Is A Good Front End Offer?

A good front end offer is a cheap "make money online" product that visitors will buy on impulse.

In general, most people are unwilling to spend anything more than $27. And are A LOT more likely to purchase in the $7-19 range.

Please note that I **do not** recommend only promoting low ticket offers. In fact, your ROI (return on investment) after you've built a relationship, will be much higher with mid-high ticket products.

The low ticket offer is best for the instant after opt-in. Where subscribers are interested in what you're showing them, but not willing to empty their pockets.

Make sense?

We need a cheap affiliate product that will get impulse buys.

Here's one that'll do the trick:

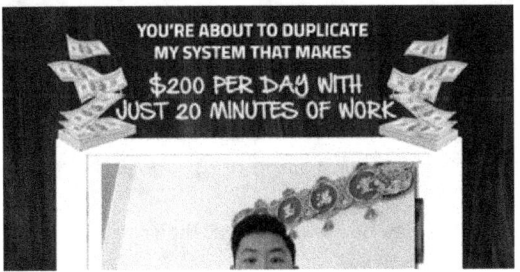

This product is called "$200 in 20 Minutes"

- It costs $9.95 (hits our low-ticket sweet spot)

- Converts at 5% (reasonable amount of visitors buy)

- Includes upsells (chances to make sales after initial purchase)

- Product title geared towards impulse buyers

All-in-all, here's a product that's a good fit for a list building funnel. There are many products just like this one, that can be found at:

- Clickbank

- JvZoo

- Warrior Plus

Each of those sites has hundreds of "make money online" products, with many income possibilities.

Imagine how much money you'll make after you have a list of people that are all interested in making money online. This is powerful stuff!

Setting Up Your Front End Offer

First off, you need an autoresponder service. Aweber is top notch and comes with a 30-day free trial.

Once you have an account at Aweber, you need to set up your web form.

These web forms can be directly installed on your website, but more likely will be integrated into some kind of fancy tool, like WP Profit Builder.

To get to the sign up forms, click on the "**Sign Up Forms**" button on your Aweber navigation bar.

Then, click on the "**Create a Sign Up Form**" button at the top right.

Save your form on the first page…

This next part is where we put our Front End Offer.

We need to grab our affiliate link. We do this by choosing an offer at Clickbank, Jvzoo or Warrior Plus and then we get our link to the chosen product with our affiliate ID attached.

That way, we make money any time someone makes a purchase with our link.

So get that link and enter it on the second page.

Next, **insert your affiliate link**. From Clickbank, Jvzoo, WarriorPlus, etc.

Click on save and move to the final page.

On the last page, click on "**I Will Install My Form**" and then click on the "**Raw HTML Version**"

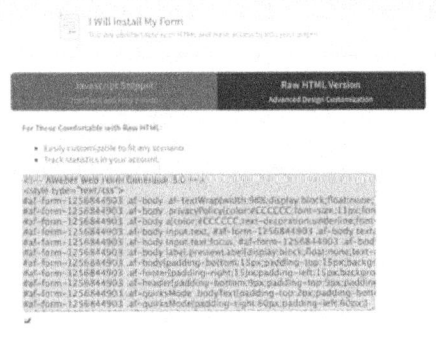

Now, you can just copy this code and place it onto your squeeze page.

This means that, when someone opt-in on your squeeze page.

You'll:

- Collect the lead

- Redirect them to your affiliate offer

In WP Profit Builder, this is really simple.

The editor has a spot on the right-hand side with the title "Form Code"

Paste the code in there and Profit Builder will take care of the rest.

Looks like this:

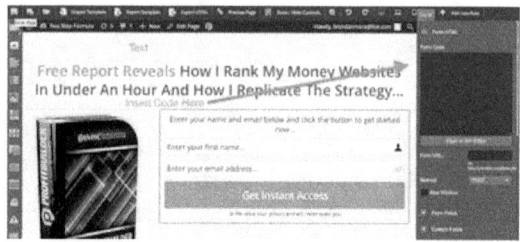

And that's it – the whole process.

Looks complicated, but it's all pretty easy once you get the hang of it!!

Easy Way to Get Traffic

Other than cold hard cash, **traffic** is your main asset. You need it. Buy it.

There are many places to buy traffic, but the **EASIEST** way is to buy solo ads.

Here's how it works:

1 You find a solo seller with a solid reputation

2 You buy an agreed upon # of clicks

3 You pay (around .40) for each click

That's it. Easy right?

Where To Find Solo Ads

There are two main places to get solo ads.

1 FaceBook

2 Skype

My preference is FaceBook. Solo sellers on FaceBook have their reputations on the line with every sale. So if you pick someone with an established rep, you're virtually guaranteed to get a decent solo.

Finding FaceBook groups that cater to solo ads is pretty darn easy. Just search for "solo ads" and you'll get a good-sized list of viable solo groups to join.

Here's the one that I own:

https://www.facebook.com/groups/189347897917735/

All of them are 100% free to join.

Find a provider with a good reputation and order your solo.

Here's a few tips, though.

- All solo traffic is pretty much the same, other than tier 1% (getting to that in a second). Don't fall for someone telling you that his traffic is way better. As someone who's purchased over 100 solos, I can say with certainty that traffic quality is comparable. The difference is how related your offer is to the traffic's interests. Ask your vendor what their list is interested in. They should be able to tell you.

- Tier 1% is an important feature. It means how much of the traffic is coming from wealthy countries. Feels weird to discriminate based on global location, but the reality is that US, UK and Canadian traffic is way more likely to actually buy things. Which at the end of the day, is your main goal.

- Prices are almost always negotiable. I've purchased dozens of solo ads and got a discount on the vast majority of them. All you gotta do is ask. Most vendors will drop their prices to close a sale. Solo vendors will be even more likely to offer a discount if you promise to write a testimonial afterwards.

Scaling Up + Making Money

Up till now, we've covered squeeze page creation and a traffic strategy that's self-replenishing.

If you keep reinvesting your front-end sales into more traffic, you'll be building your list rapidly.

Getting that big ol' email list is now a reality.

How Much Money Can You Earn With Your List?

The vast majority of the money we make should come on the back end. In marketing terms, the "back end" means all emails and promotions that occur after the initial offer.

I've heard the claim that email lists should make around $1/month per subscriber.

So let's do some quick math.

1. I have 40,000+ subscribers

2. I make about $5,000 a month (from my list)

Okay, so clearly not $1 a month for me. The reality is that there are loads of variables that affect your income per subscriber.

There are marketers with higher earnings per subscriber and marketers with much lower. It's going to depend completely on how you market to them.

The reality though, is that this is about as easy as it gets to make money online. But more on that later.

The Money Is In The Email Sequence

The front end offer enables us to keep reinvesting in more traffic. Which gives us our email list.

The autoresponder sequence is where we make the big bucks.

An autoresponder sequence is a series of emails that are sent to your list after they initially opt-in.

Most autoresponder services, like Aweber, allow you to build it as big and robust as you want. It's a good idea to have a full sequence ready to go.

Here's the first 5 emails in my sequence:

My Aweber sequence currently has 124 follow-up emails. And I still keep adding to it.

The sequence MUST have promotions but it **ALSO** must _add value_ to your subscribers. If you only send promotions, it won't take long for you to burn through your leads.

Burning a list means that subscribers no longer open your emails or click on your links. It's a very bad thing. And it's easily avoidable by adding some value in between your promotions.

My email sequence has a nice balance of value submissions and offers. It's taken me awhile to put together and tweak, but it's been worth it.

Want To Get A Head Start?

Aweber allows marketers to share their email sequences with each other.

It's a badass feature that really does not get used enough in our market.

I'm about to share with you my entire email sequence. All 120+ emails, completely done-for-you.

To get my email sequence, you just need to

1. Sign up for a 30-day free trial at Aweber

2. Paste in my "campaign share code"

Campaign Code = awlist4148279-5b487-$F

You just need to copy the sharing code you get above and place it here:

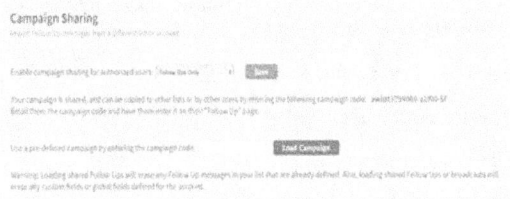

Right where it says "Use a pre-defined campaign by entering the campaign code:"

Paste in the code and it'll upload my entire sequence.

What You Need To Change?

It is not recommended to use these emails "out of the box" so to speak.

There are a few changes to be made-

Change The Branding

These emails use the "Brendan Mace" branding a lot, Especially, at the end the messages. Just go in there and edit the text. Personalize to your name (or company).

Change The Affiliate Links

As it stands right now, the links all have my affiliate ID attached.

This is a really simple fix. All of the products promoted are either from the Clickbank Marketplace or JvZoo. Find out which each product belongs to and get your own affiliate link.

This is crucial. You need your affiliate links in there to make the money.

Add Your Own Stuff

Your funnel is (and should be) different than mine. Add your own stuff in here. Whether that's blog posts, or affiliate promotions. You get to pick where the traffic goes.

Make The Content Unique

If you really want to go the extra mile then you should go through each email and rewrite it so it's unique.

You don't have to write them from scratch, just look at what I have written then tweak it so it says the same thing but in slightly different words.

How Much Can I Make Per Hour?

Here's a list building MYTH that never gets old. I see questions, like *"how much can I make [in 'x' amount of time] from now?"*

This myth makes sense, I mean, people are used to working in 9-5 jobs and expect their income to match the time and effort put in.

It doesn't work like that. For better or for worse.

There are only three metrics that matter!!

> 1. How much do you EARN per visitor
>
> 2. How much are you paying per visitor
>
> 3. How much traffic did you buy

Here's a thought provoking question for ya...

If I told you that for every $1 you gave me, I'd give you $2 back.

How many dollars would you give me?

If you were smart, you'd give me near every dollar you have. Because you'd know that for every $1, you'd get $2 back.

The key is to build a funnel that makes more per visitor than you spend on traffic. If you can do that, you've won!!

Here's a time breakdown for you:

> • buying traffic takes 10 minutes
>
> • writing an email to send takes 10 minutes

And BOOM... That's it.

20 minutes total.

Once you have a funnel in place, you can literally spend 20 minutes per day on this and easily make a full time income. No joke!!

Living The Laptop Lifestyle

Your most valuable currency is not money – it's time.

Sadly, the 9-5 job-lifestyle swallows it all up. After getting ready for work, commuting to the job and taking care of household chores, most 9-5'ers are left with an hour or less of free time.

What's the point of making money without any *time* to spend it on?

The real advantage of this "20 minute" routine is that it'll give you all the money you need to pay your bills, take that long awaited vacation, provide for your family, even some extra cash to burn on fun.

You can start to live the laptop lifestyle.

Most importantly, though, this business model will give you time.

… What you do with that time is up to you.

But here's some ideas:

- Travel

- Learn a language

- Fall in love

- Stay in love

- Time with your kids

- Improve your funnel

It's not healthy to do all work and no play. You need a balance between the two. And sometimes, you just need to take a break from work altogether and enjoy a well earned vacation

Here's some pictures of my trip to Cuba:

Setting up a passive income business model gives you **FREEDOM!**

Even while you're on a beach in Cuba...

Aweber is still sending mail to your subscribers. That means you're making money 24/7/365. And it only takes about 20 minutes of your time a day to keep it all growing.

Bonus Traffic Strategy

So far, I've advised *buying* traffic through solo ads. There is a FREE method, though.

Once you get 800-1000+ subscribers, you can start *trading clicks.*

This works very similarly to buying solo ads. Instead of paying for traffic, you just deliver traffic to a partners page and in turn, get the same amount of clicks back.

It's easy.

How Click Banking Works

1) Go to a clickbanking FaceBook group.

– "Clickbanking" is a fancy word for trading clicks. That's all you need to know.

There's a group here, here and here.

2) Find 5 FaceBook members with several testimonials

– There are TONS to choose from

3) Ask them if they would like to bank clicks with you.

– Make sure to be willing to send first. If you're the newbie on the block and you're contacting established banking partners, its good banking etiquette to send first.

Okay, got some banking partners. Now what?

Your banking partners will give you a *tracking link*. This is how they'll know how many clicks you've sent to their offer.

You also need to create a "trackable link," so that you can send the appropriate amount of clicks to their page.

A free service for link tracking is called Bit.Ly. It's not the best and I'd recommend investing in a better one later. But for just starting out – it'll do the job just fine!!

Then it's easy.

Write up a broadcast email in your Aweber account and include the link to your partner's offer.

Once you've hit the agreed upon # of clicks. Contact your partner and give them a link to YOUR offer.

For Example

You could arrange to bank 100 clicks with 5 partners. Every time you finish sending 100 clicks to a partner, you move on to the next one.

After all is said and done. You'll have sent out around 500 clicks to your partners.

In turn, they'll owe you 500 clicks back. That's **500 FREE visitors** that you don't have to buy.

If you were purchasing a solo ad, that much traffic would cost you about **$200.**

Trading clicks with banking partners is a great way to get FREE traffic.

Package all of this together, and you can easily build a $200/day passive income stream with list building.

Now go do it!

Conclusion – Wrapping it Up

This book has given you options. Five great ways to make passive income that all work for you, so that you don't have to work forever.

If you find videos easier to follow than reading, I've created a 3-Part YouTube series right here on how I make passive income online. You'll see everything over my shoulder as I go through my main business model.

I hope you enjoyed reading about my passive income strategies.

My last piece of advice is this: Don't let *small minds* convince you that your dreams are TOO BIG.

You can do this!!

If you would like to learn more about how to build passive income online, then I would love to chat with you. Check out my blog that shares in depth guides, like this one.

Right here: www.brendanmace.com

FREE 20 Minute Coaching Call

~No Gimmicks. No Catches~

Click Here to Claim